ASSASSIN'S CREED ™

4 | HAWK

STORY : CORBEYRAN
ART : DJILLALI DEFALI
COLOR : CYRIL VINCENT

Also available
1. DESMOND
2. AQUILUS
3. ACCIPITER

ASSASSIN'S CREED: HAWK
ISBN: 9781781168394

Published by Titan Books
A division of Titan Publishing Group Ltd.
144 Southwark Street, London SE1 0UP

First Titan edition: November 2013
English-language translation: Mark McKenzie-Ray

A CIP catalogue record for this title is available from the British Library

10 9 8 7 6 5 4 3 2 1

Printed in China

*The authors wish to thank David Roberts, whose pictures
were an inspiration for the scenes in Egypt.*

What did you think of this book? We love to hear from our readers. Please email us
at: readerfeedback@titanemail.com, or write to us at the above address. To receive
advance information, news, competitions, and exclusive offers online, please sign up
for the Titan newsletter on our website: www.titanbooks.com

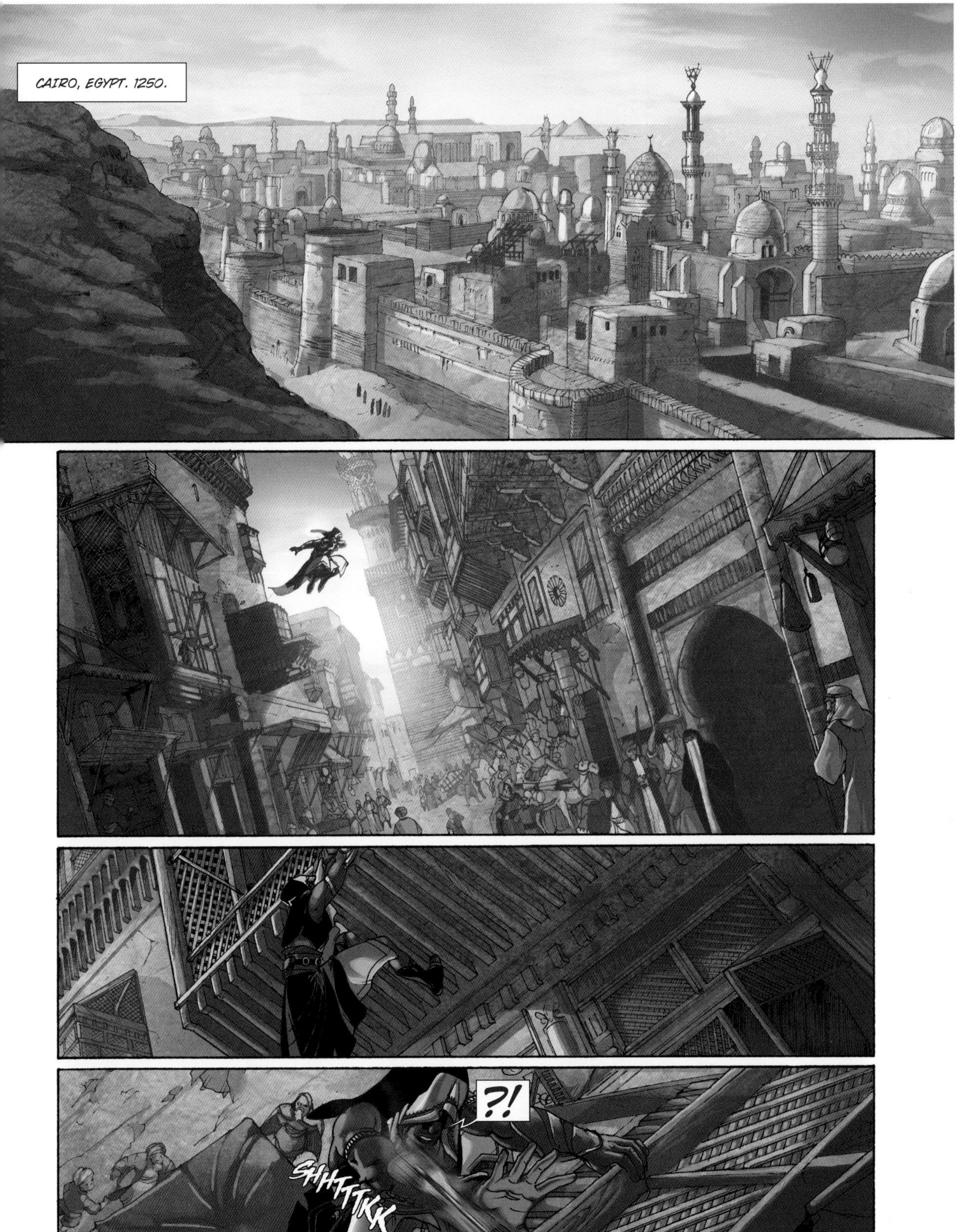
CAIRO, EGYPT. 1250.
?!
SHHTTTKK

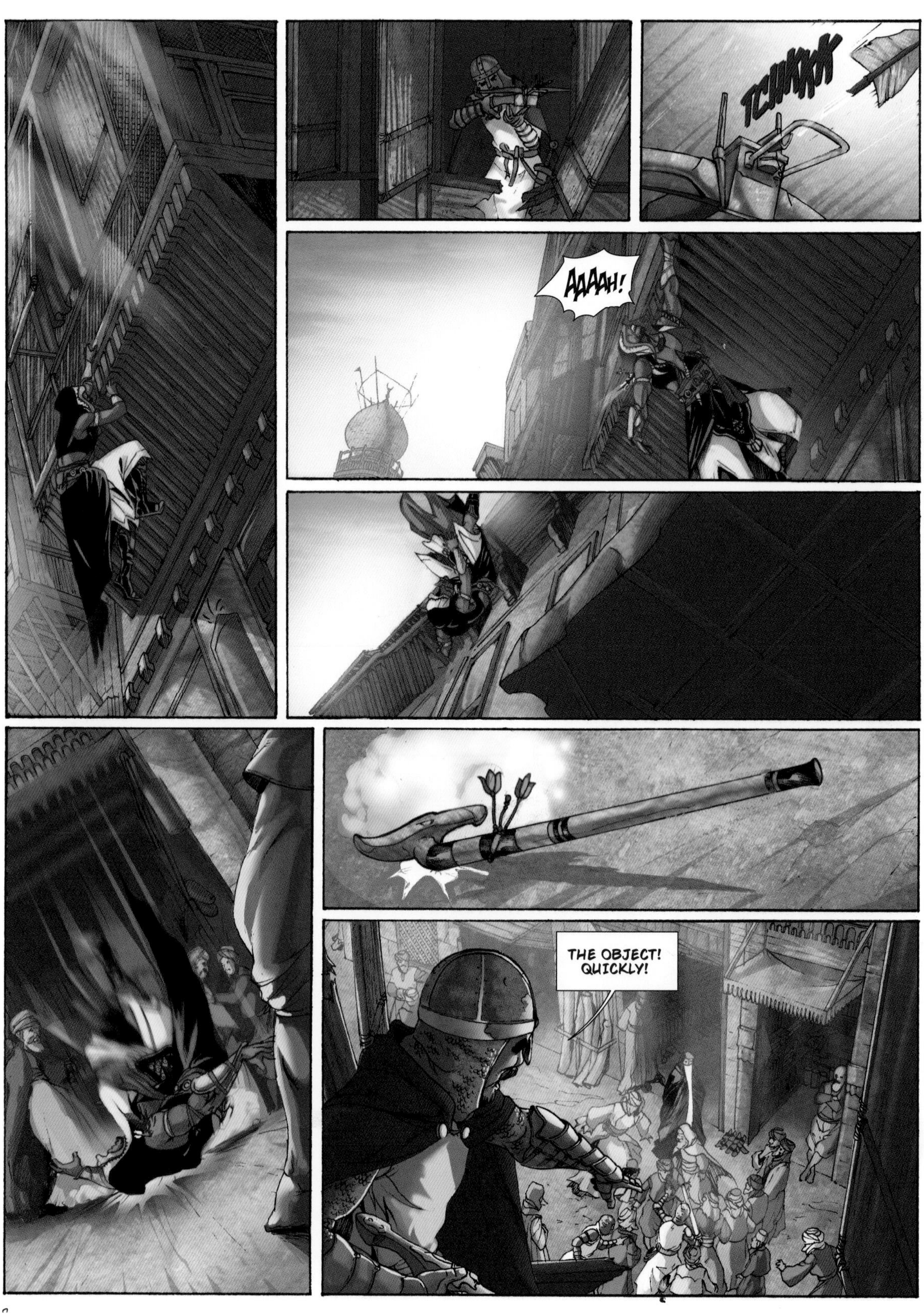
TCHKKKK
AAAAH!
THE OBJECT! QUICKLY!

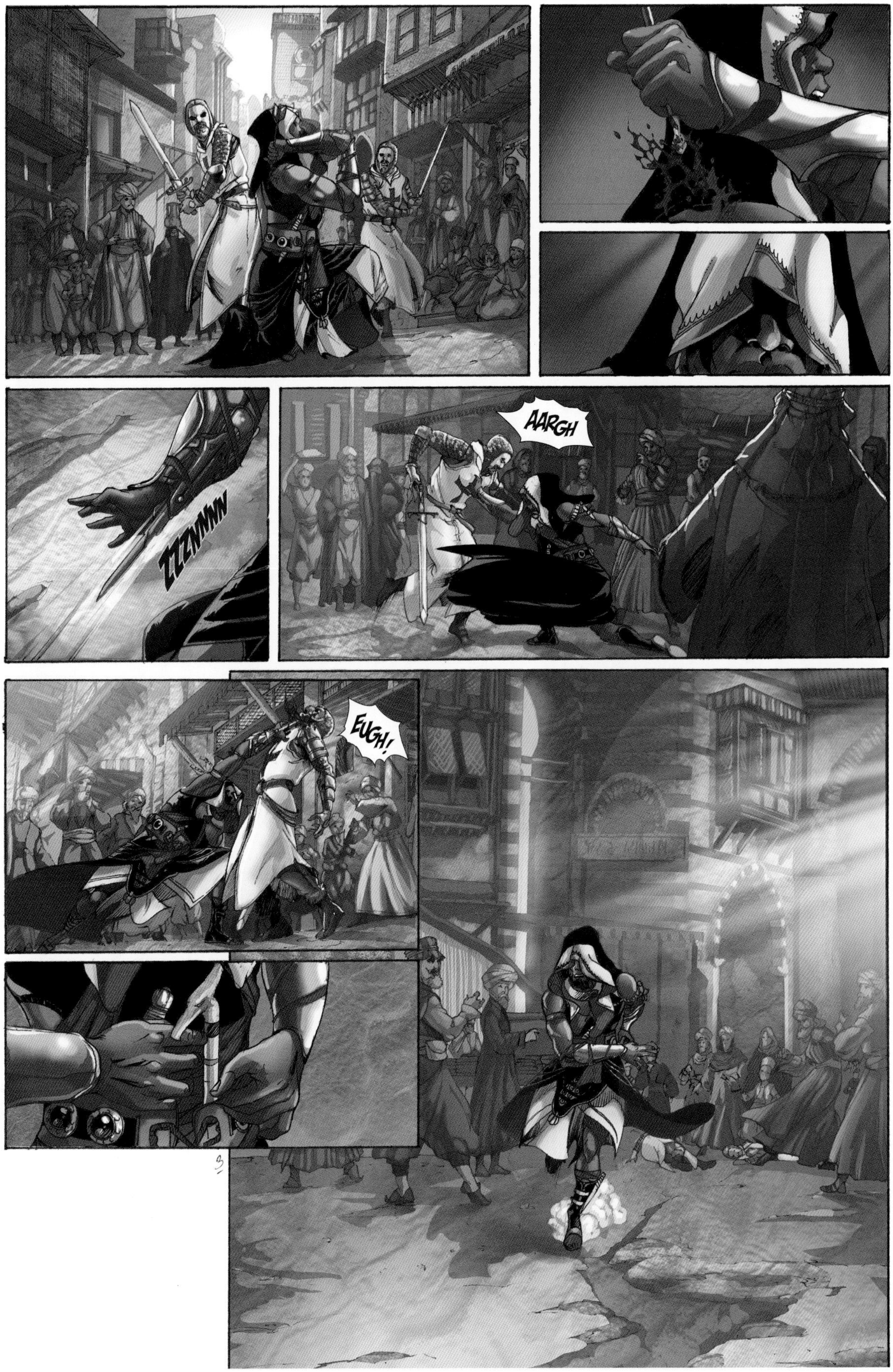
ZZZNNNN
AARGH
EUGH!

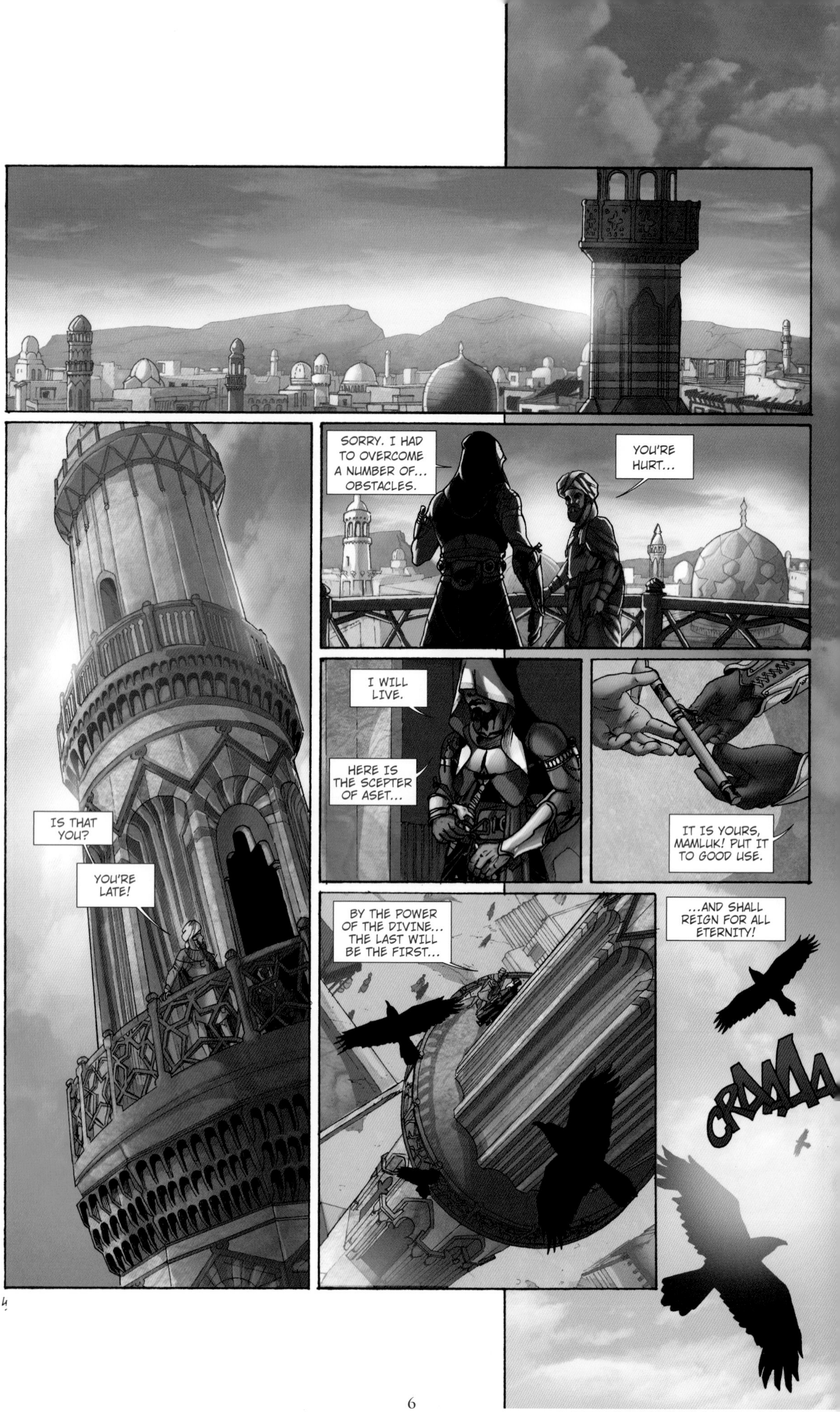
IS THAT YOU?
YOU'RE LATE!
SORRY. I HAD TO OVERCOME A NUMBER OF... OBSTACLES.
YOU'RE HURT...
I WILL LIVE.
HERE IS THE SCEPTER OF ASET...
IT IS YOURS, MAMLUK! PUT IT TO GOOD USE.
BY THE POWER OF THE DIVINE... THE LAST WILL BE THE FIRST...
...AND SHALL REIGN FOR ALL ETERNITY!
CRAAAA

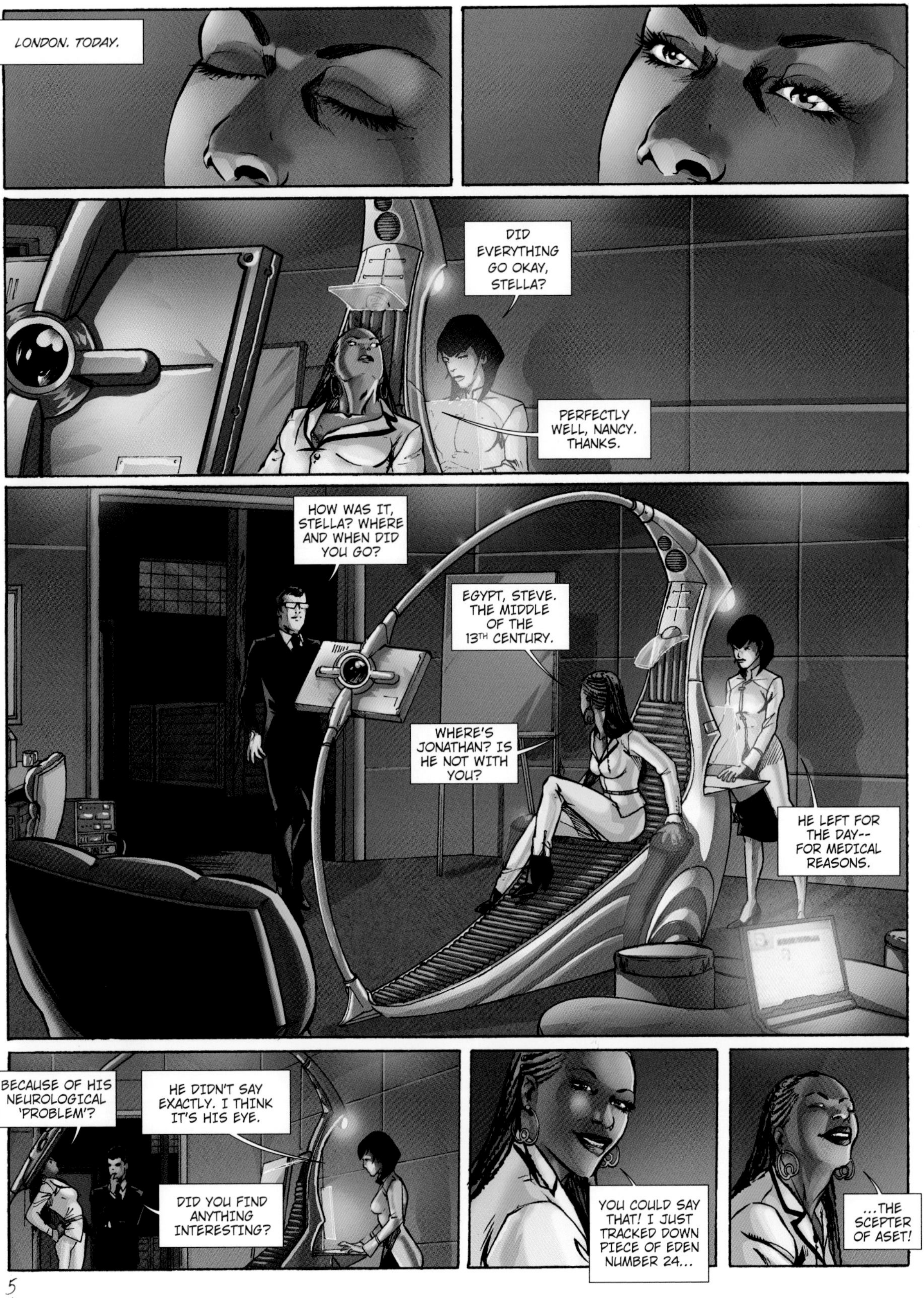
LONDON. TODAY.
DID EVERYTHING GO OKAY, STELLA?
PERFECTLY WELL, NANCY. THANKS.
HOW WAS IT, STELLA? WHERE AND WHEN DID YOU GO?
EGYPT, STEVE. THE MIDDLE OF THE 13TH CENTURY.
WHERE'S JONATHAN? IS HE NOT WITH YOU?
HE LEFT FOR THE DAY-- FOR MEDICAL REASONS.
BECAUSE OF HIS NEUROLOGICAL 'PROBLEM'?
HE DIDN'T SAY EXACTLY. I THINK IT'S HIS EYE.
DID YOU FIND ANYTHING INTERESTING?
YOU COULD SAY THAT! I JUST TRACKED DOWN PIECE OF EDEN NUMBER 24...
...THE SCEPTER OF ASET!

5

IF MY MEMORY SERVES, THIS ISN'T THE FIRST TIME ONE OF YOUR ANCESTORS HAS CROSSED PATHS WITH THIS OBJECT.

YOU'RE RIGHT. WE'VE MANAGED TO TRACE BITS AND PIECES OF ITS HISTORY BEFORE.

"ACCORDING TO OUR RECORDS, IT SEEMS THAT THE SCEPTER ORIGINALLY BELONGED TO THE GODDESS ISIS--THE GREEK NAME FOR ASET. SHE WAS ONE OF THE MOST INFLUENTIAL FIGURES FROM THE 'FIRST CIVILIZATION'.

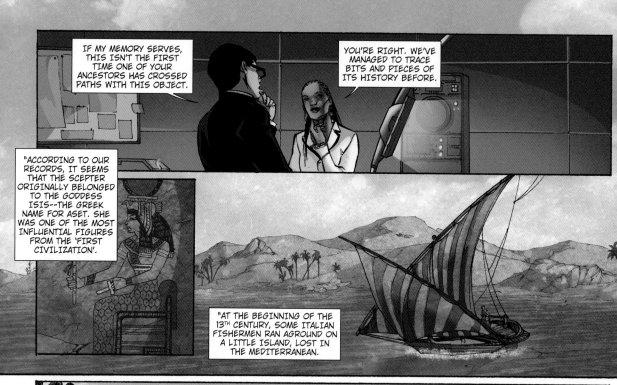

"AT THE BEGINNING OF THE 13TH CENTURY, SOME ITALIAN FISHERMEN RAN AGROUND ON A LITTLE ISLAND, LOST IN THE MEDITERRANEAN.

"THEY FOUND THE SCEPTER HIDDEN AMONG THE DEBRIS OF A BOAT THAT HAD BEEN SHIPWRECKED SEVERAL CENTURIES BEFORE.

"THEY ALSO FOUND A BRONZE BELT BUCKLE AMONGST THE WRECKAGE.

"ENGRAVED IN THE METAL OF THE BUCKLE WAS THE SHAPE OF A CROW."

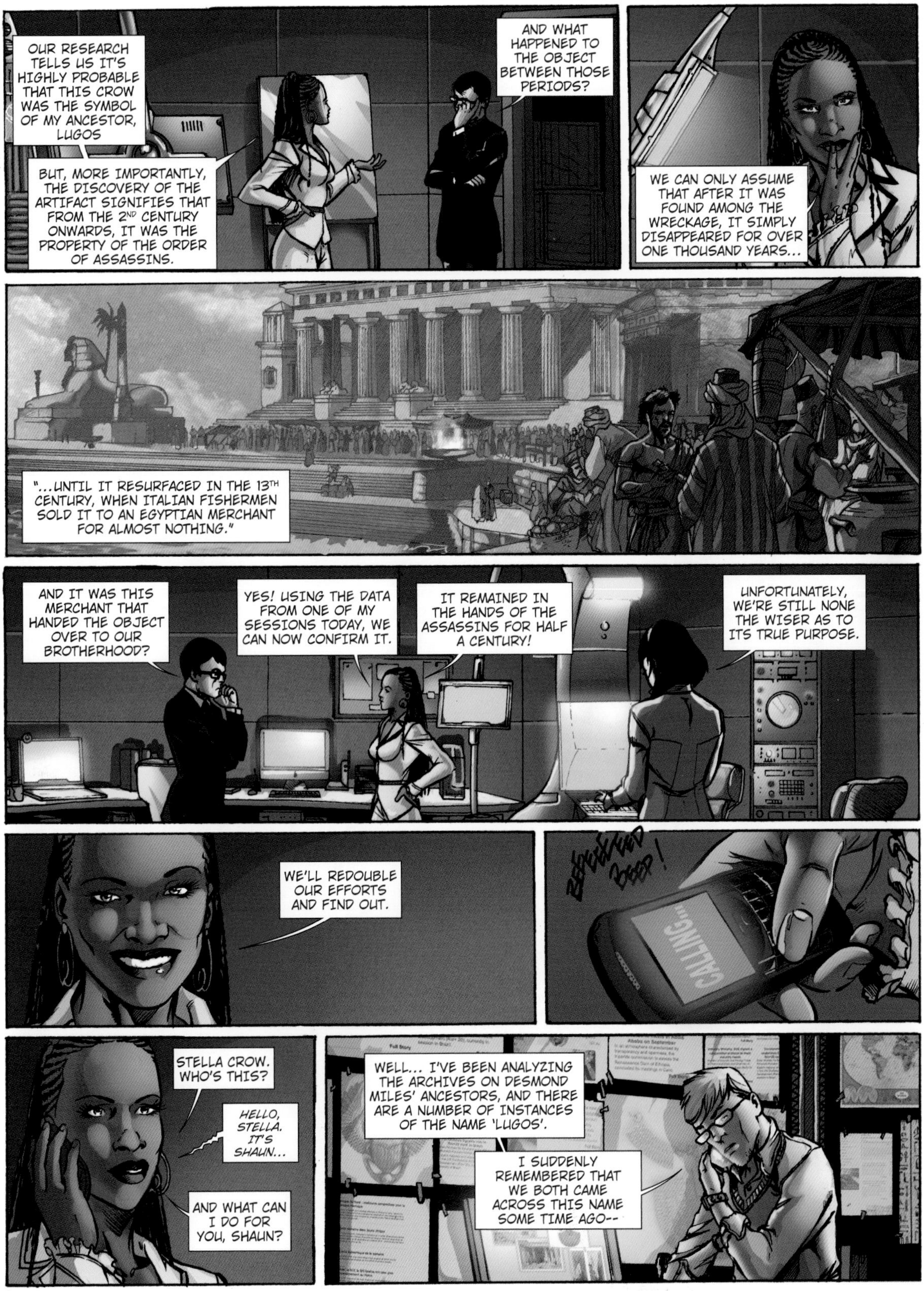
OUR RESEARCH TELLS US IT'S HIGHLY PROBABLE THAT THIS CROW WAS THE SYMBOL OF MY ANCESTOR, LUGOS
BUT, MORE IMPORTANTLY, THE DISCOVERY OF THE ARTIFACT SIGNIFIES THAT FROM THE 2ND CENTURY ONWARDS, IT WAS THE PROPERTY OF THE ORDER OF ASSASSINS.
AND WHAT HAPPENED TO THE OBJECT BETWEEN THOSE PERIODS?
WE CAN ONLY ASSUME THAT AFTER IT WAS FOUND AMONG THE WRECKAGE, IT SIMPLY DISAPPEARED FOR OVER ONE THOUSAND YEARS...
"...UNTIL IT RESURFACED IN THE 13TH CENTURY, WHEN ITALIAN FISHERMEN SOLD IT TO AN EGYPTIAN MERCHANT FOR ALMOST NOTHING."
AND IT WAS THIS MERCHANT THAT HANDED THE OBJECT OVER TO OUR BROTHERHOOD?
YES! USING THE DATA FROM ONE OF MY SESSIONS TODAY, WE CAN NOW CONFIRM IT.
IT REMAINED IN THE HANDS OF THE ASSASSINS FOR HALF A CENTURY!
UNFORTUNATELY, WE'RE STILL NONE THE WISER AS TO ITS TRUE PURPOSE.
WE'LL REDOUBLE OUR EFFORTS AND FIND OUT.
CALLING...
STELLA CROW. WHO'S THIS?
HELLO, STELLA. IT'S SHAUN...
AND WHAT CAN I DO FOR YOU, SHAUN?
WELL... I'VE BEEN ANALYZING THE ARCHIVES ON DESMOND MILES' ANCESTORS, AND THERE ARE A NUMBER OF INSTANCES OF THE NAME 'LUGOS'.
I SUDDENLY REMEMBERED THAT WE BOTH CAME ACROSS THIS NAME SOME TIME AGO--

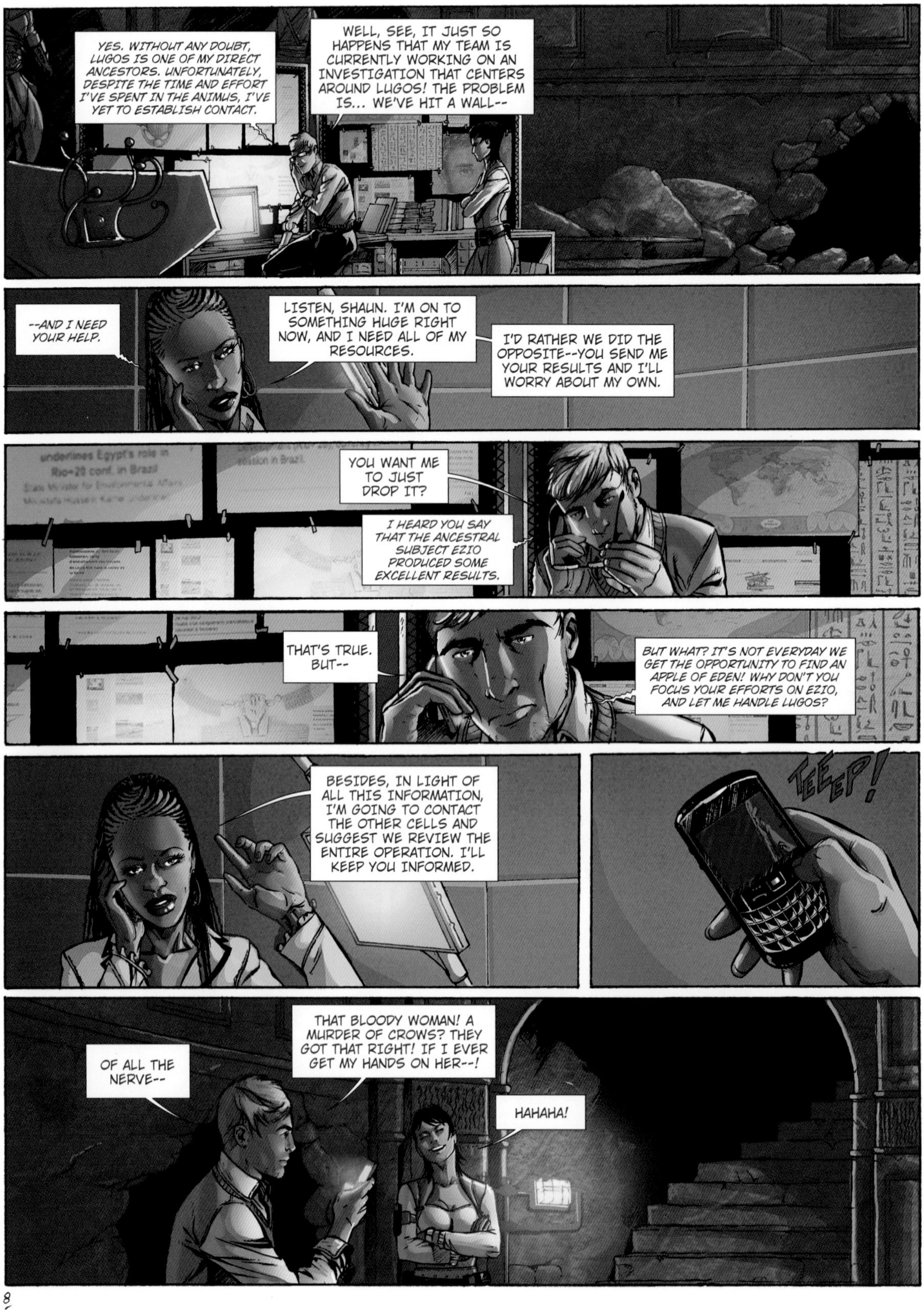
YES. WITHOUT ANY DOUBT, LUGOS IS ONE OF MY DIRECT ANCESTORS. UNFORTUNATELY, DESPITE THE TIME AND EFFORT I'VE SPENT IN THE ANIMUS, I'VE YET TO ESTABLISH CONTACT.
WELL, SEE, IT JUST SO HAPPENS THAT MY TEAM IS CURRENTLY WORKING ON AN INVESTIGATION THAT CENTERS AROUND LUGOS! THE PROBLEM IS... WE'VE HIT A WALL--
--AND I NEED YOUR HELP.
LISTEN, SHAUN. I'M ON TO SOMETHING HUGE RIGHT NOW, AND I NEED ALL OF MY RESOURCES.
I'D RATHER WE DID THE OPPOSITE--YOU SEND ME YOUR RESULTS AND I'LL WORRY ABOUT MY OWN.
YOU WANT ME TO JUST DROP IT?
I HEARD YOU SAY THAT THE ANCESTRAL SUBJECT EZIO PRODUCED SOME EXCELLENT RESULTS.
THAT'S TRUE. BUT--
BUT WHAT? IT'S NOT EVERYDAY WE GET THE OPPORTUNITY TO FIND AN APPLE OF EDEN! WHY DON'T YOU FOCUS YOUR EFFORTS ON EZIO, AND LET ME HANDLE LUGOS?
BESIDES, IN LIGHT OF ALL THIS INFORMATION, I'M GOING TO CONTACT THE OTHER CELLS AND SUGGEST WE REVIEW THE ENTIRE OPERATION. I'LL KEEP YOU INFORMED.
TEEEP!
OF ALL THE NERVE--
THAT BLOODY WOMAN! A MURDER OF CROWS? THEY GOT THAT RIGHT! IF I EVER GET MY HANDS ON HER--!
HAHAHA!
8

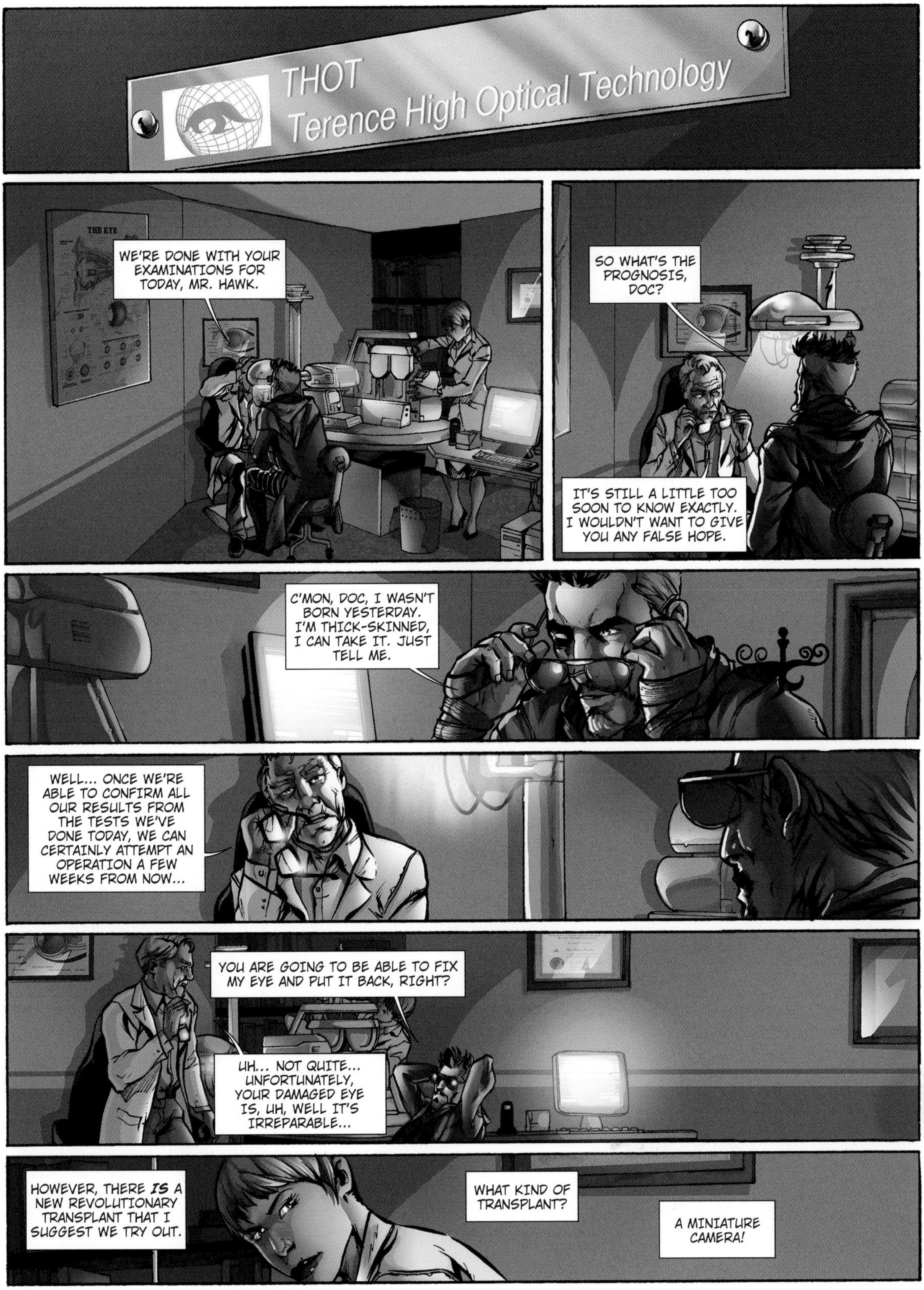
THOT
Terence High Optical Technology
WE'RE DONE WITH YOUR EXAMINATIONS FOR TODAY, MR. HAWK.
SO WHAT'S THE PROGNOSIS, DOC?
IT'S STILL A LITTLE TOO SOON TO KNOW EXACTLY. I WOULDN'T WANT TO GIVE YOU ANY FALSE HOPE.
C'MON, DOC, I WASN'T BORN YESTERDAY. I'M THICK-SKINNED, I CAN TAKE IT. JUST TELL ME.
WELL... ONCE WE'RE ABLE TO CONFIRM ALL OUR RESULTS FROM THE TESTS WE'VE DONE TODAY, WE CAN CERTAINLY ATTEMPT AN OPERATION A FEW WEEKS FROM NOW...
YOU ARE GOING TO BE ABLE TO FIX MY EYE AND PUT IT BACK, RIGHT?
UH... NOT QUITE... UNFORTUNATELY, YOUR DAMAGED EYE IS, UH, WELL IT'S IRREPARABLE...
HOWEVER, THERE IS A NEW REVOLUTIONARY TRANSPLANT THAT I SUGGEST WE TRY OUT.
WHAT KIND OF TRANSPLANT?
A MINIATURE CAMERA!

9

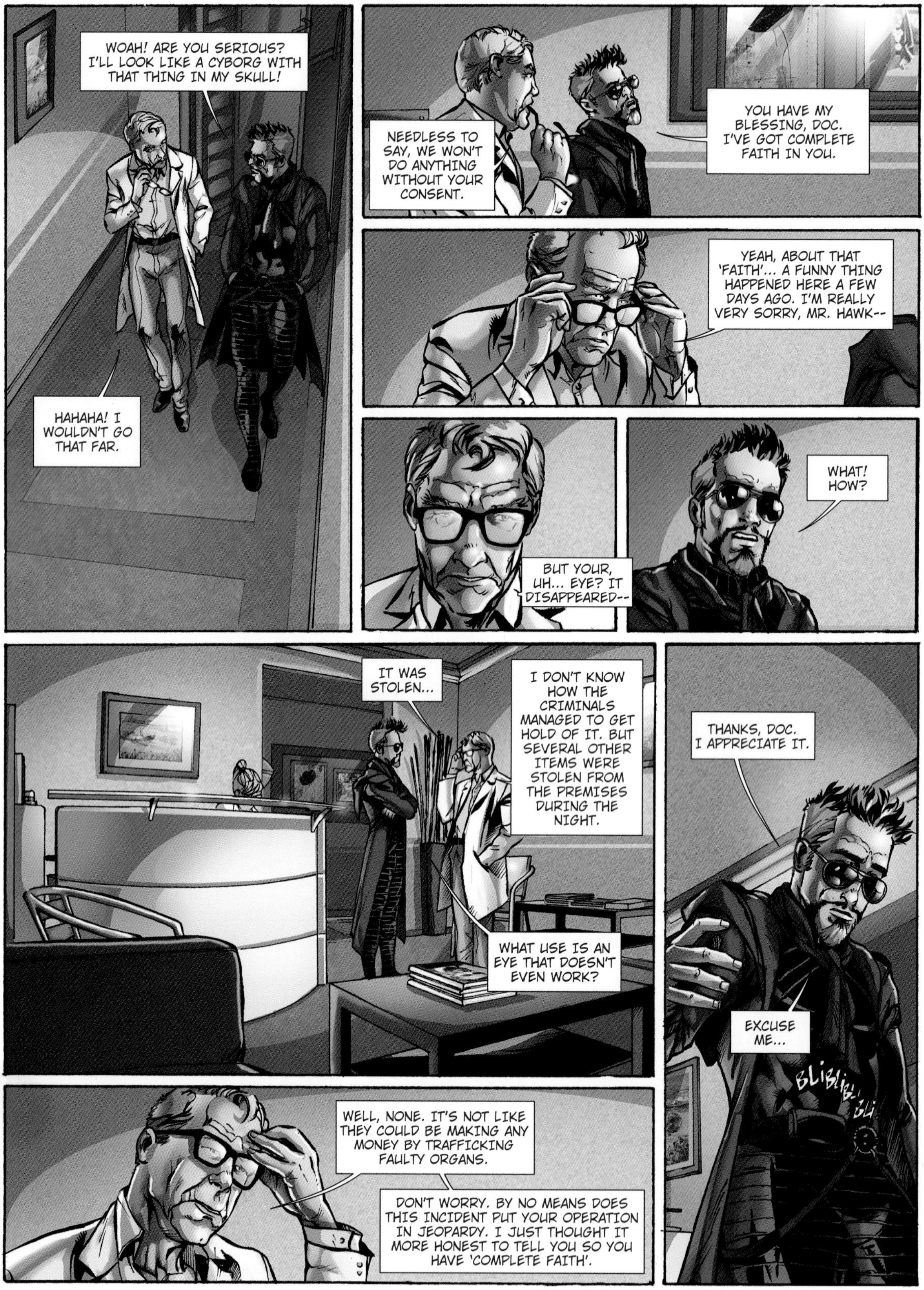
WOAH! ARE YOU SERIOUS? I'LL LOOK LIKE A CYBORG WITH THAT THING IN MY SKULL!
HAHAHA! I WOULDN'T GO THAT FAR.
NEEDLESS TO SAY, WE WON'T DO ANYTHING WITHOUT YOUR CONSENT.
YOU HAVE MY BLESSING, DOC. I'VE GOT COMPLETE FAITH IN YOU.
YEAH, ABOUT THAT 'FAITH'... A FUNNY THING HAPPENED HERE A FEW DAYS AGO. I'M REALLY VERY SORRY, MR. HAWK--
BUT YOUR, UH... EYE? IT DISAPPEARED--
WHAT! HOW?
IT WAS STOLEN...
I DON'T KNOW HOW THE CRIMINALS MANAGED TO GET HOLD OF IT. BUT SEVERAL OTHER ITEMS WERE STOLEN FROM THE PREMISES DURING THE NIGHT.
WHAT USE IS AN EYE THAT DOESN'T EVEN WORK?
WELL, NONE. IT'S NOT LIKE THEY COULD BE MAKING ANY MONEY BY TRAFFICKING FAULTY ORGANS.
DON'T WORRY. BY NO MEANS DOES THIS INCIDENT PUT YOUR OPERATION IN JEOPARDY. I JUST THOUGHT IT MORE HONEST TO TELL YOU SO YOU HAVE 'COMPLETE FAITH'.
THANKS, DOC. I APPRECIATE IT.
EXCUSE ME...
BLIBLIBLIBLI

10

HAWK. SHOOT.

JONATHAN. IT'S STELLA... ARE YOU FREE? CAN YOU TALK?

YEAH, I'M JUST ON MY WAY OUT.

I NEED YOU TO JUMP ON THE NEXT PLANE TO ITALY AND MEET UP WITH LUCY AND SHAUN AS QUICKLY AS YOU CAN...

NO PROBLEM. WHEREABOUTS IN ITALY?

I'LL ENCODE THEIR COORDINATES AND SEND THEM TO YOU. MAKE SURE YOU DELETE THE DATA WHEN YOU'RE DONE.

OKAY, AND ONCE I'M THERE, THEN WHAT?

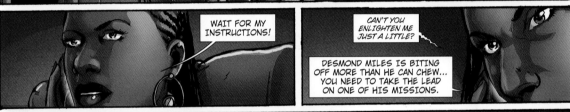

WAIT FOR MY INSTRUCTIONS!

CAN'T YOU ENLIGHTEN ME JUST A LITTLE?

DESMOND MILES IS BITING OFF MORE THAN HE CAN CHEW... YOU NEED TO TAKE THE LEAD ON ONE OF HIS MISSIONS.

LISTEN, JONATHAN. THIS MISSION IS IMPORTANT. IT'S CENTERED AROUND LUGOS, ONE OF MY ANCESTORS. I'VE NEVER HAD THE OPPORTUNITY TO EXPLORE HIS PAST BEFORE, NOT VIA MY GENETIC MEMORY. I'VE GOT A LOT RIDING ON THIS, NOT JUST PROFESSIONALLY--

SO THIS A PERSONAL MATTER?

I'M IN NO MOOD FOR YOUR QUESTIONS, JON! ALL I'M ASKING YOU TO DO IS FOLLOW MY INSTRUCTIONS!

ALL RIGHT, STELLA, CHILL OUT. I'M JUST KIDDING. I'M ALL OVER IT.

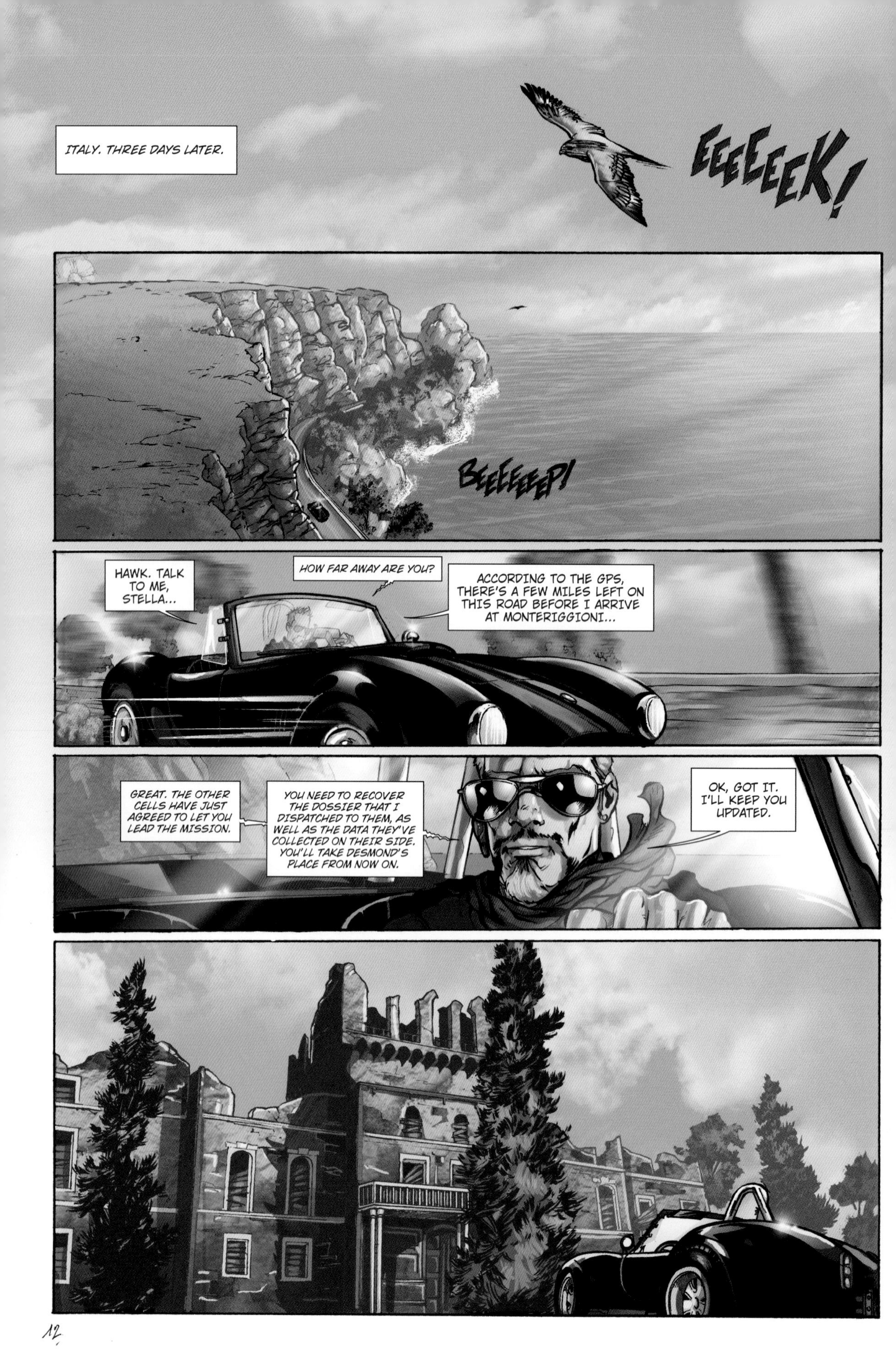

ITALY. THREE DAYS LATER.
EEEEEEK!
BEEEEEEP!
HAWK. TALK TO ME, STELLA...
HOW FAR AWAY ARE YOU?
ACCORDING TO THE GPS, THERE'S A FEW MILES LEFT ON THIS ROAD BEFORE I ARRIVE AT MONTERIGGIONI...
GREAT. THE OTHER CELLS HAVE JUST AGREED TO LET YOU LEAD THE MISSION.
YOU NEED TO RECOVER THE DOSSIER THAT I DISPATCHED TO THEM, AS WELL AS THE DATA THEY'VE COLLECTED ON THEIR SIDE. YOU'LL TAKE DESMOND'S PLACE FROM NOW ON.
OK, GOT IT. I'LL KEEP YOU UPDATED.
12

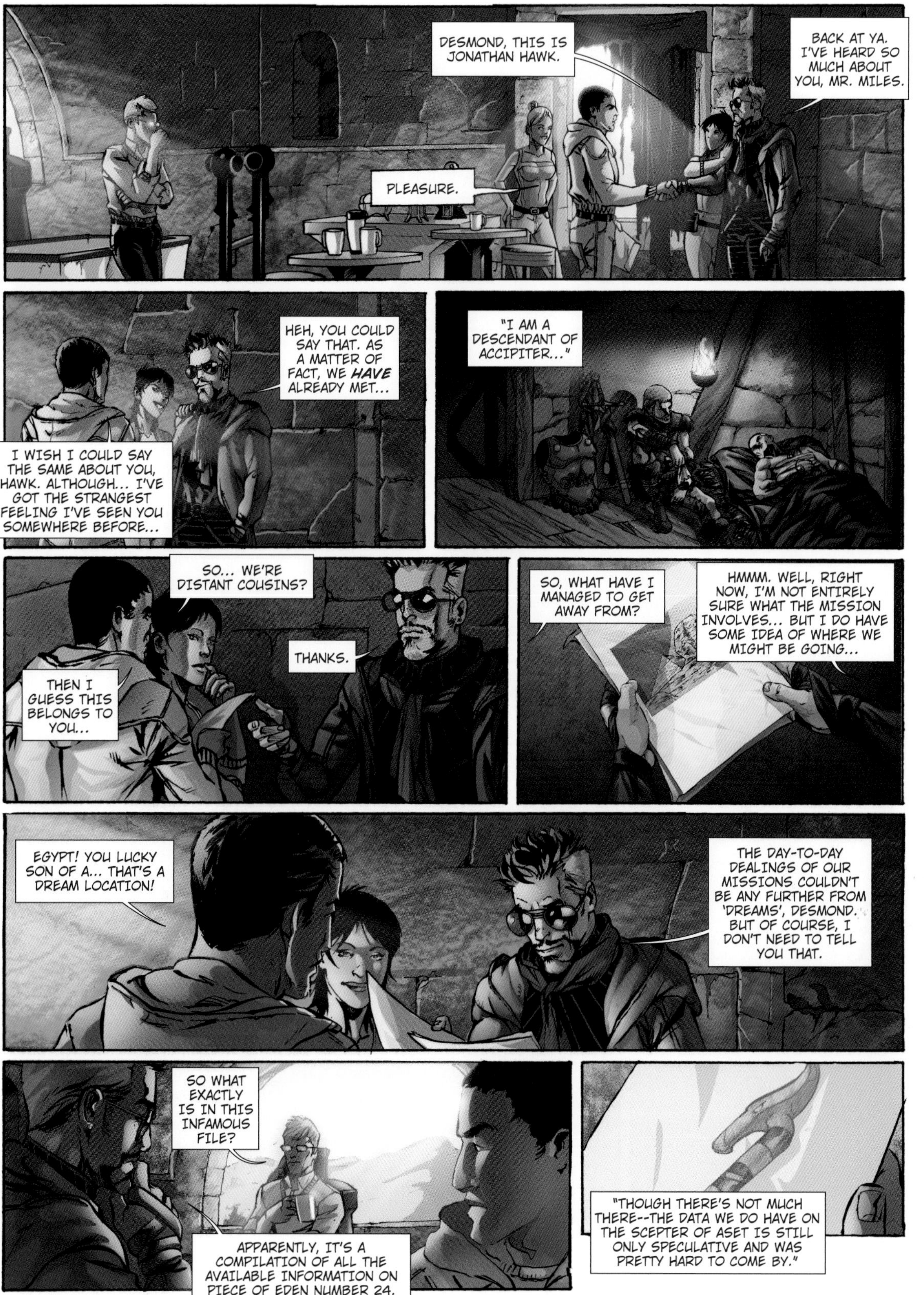
DESMOND, THIS IS JONATHAN HAWK.
BACK AT YA. I'VE HEARD SO MUCH ABOUT YOU, MR. MILES.
PLEASURE.
HEH, YOU COULD SAY THAT. AS A MATTER OF FACT, WE *HAVE* ALREADY MET...
I WISH I COULD SAY THE SAME ABOUT YOU, HAWK. ALTHOUGH... I'VE GOT THE STRANGEST FEELING I'VE SEEN YOU SOMEWHERE BEFORE...
"I AM A DESCENDANT OF ACCIPITER..."
SO... WE'RE DISTANT COUSINS?
THANKS.
THEN I GUESS THIS BELONGS TO YOU...
SO, WHAT HAVE I MANAGED TO GET AWAY FROM?
HMMM. WELL, RIGHT NOW, I'M NOT ENTIRELY SURE WHAT THE MISSION INVOLVES... BUT I DO HAVE SOME IDEA OF WHERE WE MIGHT BE GOING...
EGYPT! YOU LUCKY SON OF A... THAT'S A DREAM LOCATION!
THE DAY-TO-DAY DEALINGS OF OUR MISSIONS COULDN'T BE ANY FURTHER FROM 'DREAMS', DESMOND. BUT OF COURSE, I DON'T NEED TO TELL YOU THAT.
SO WHAT EXACTLY IS IN THIS INFAMOUS FILE?
APPARENTLY, IT'S A COMPILATION OF ALL THE AVAILABLE INFORMATION ON PIECE OF EDEN NUMBER 24.
"THOUGH THERE'S NOT MUCH THERE--THE DATA WE DO HAVE ON THE SCEPTER OF ASET IS STILL ONLY SPECULATIVE AND WAS PRETTY HARD TO COME BY."

13

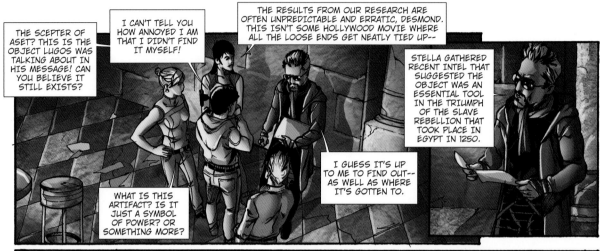

THE SCEPTER OF ASET? THIS IS THE OBJECT LUGOS WAS TALKING ABOUT IN HIS MESSAGE! CAN YOU BELIEVE IT STILL EXISTS?

I CAN'T TELL YOU HOW ANNOYED I AM THAT I DIDN'T FIND IT MYSELF!

THE RESULTS FROM OUR RESEARCH ARE OFTEN UNPREDICTABLE AND ERRATIC, DESMOND. THIS ISN'T SOME HOLLYWOOD MOVIE WHERE ALL THE LOOSE ENDS GET NEATLY TIED UP--

STELLA GATHERED RECENT INTEL THAT SUGGESTED THE OBJECT WAS AN ESSENTIAL TOOL IN THE TRIUMPH OF THE SLAVE REBELLION THAT TOOK PLACE IN EGYPT IN 1250.

WHAT IS THIS ARTIFACT? IS IT JUST A SYMBOL OF POWER? OR SOMETHING MORE?

I GUESS IT'S UP TO ME TO FIND OUT-- AS WELL AS WHERE IT'S GOTTEN TO.

"THIS REBELLION WAS A MAJOR EVENT. IT MARKED THE END OF THE TYRANNY OF THE AYYUBID DYNASTY.

"FOLLOWING THE UPRISING OF THE MAMLUKS, THE BAHRI DYNASTY WAS ESTABLISHED IN EGYPT.

"THANKS TO THE GODDESS' SCEPTER, THE SLAVES BECAME THE MASTERS."

BY THE POWER OF THE DIVINE, THE LAST WILL BE THE FIRST AND SHALL REIGN FOR ALL ETERNITY!

"IT'S ALMOST CERTAIN THAT OUR BROTHERHOOD ENCOURAGED THE SLAVES TO REBEL AGAINST THEIR MASTERS AND HELPED THEM TO SEIZE POWER BY USING THIS OBJECT.

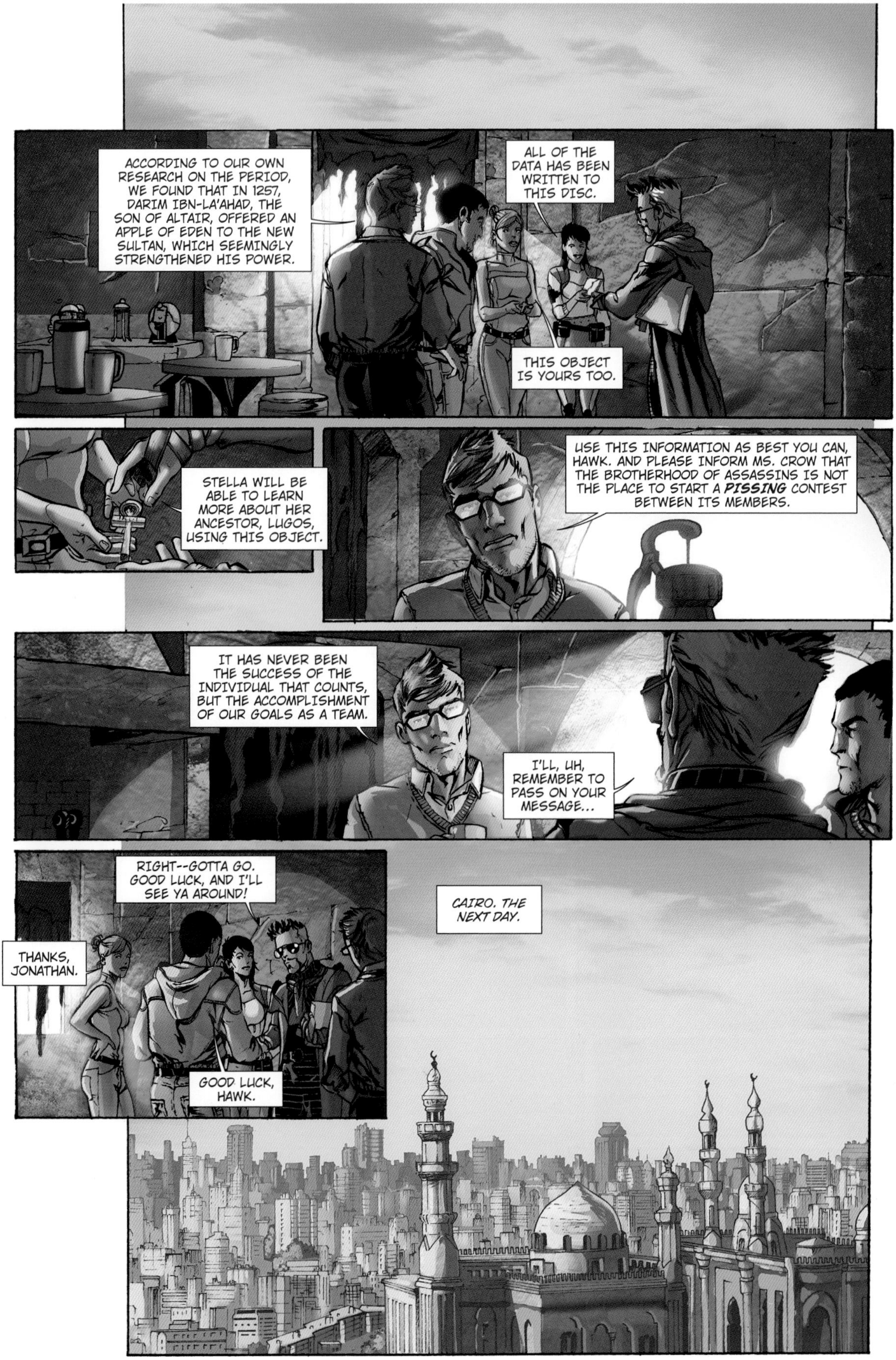

ACCORDING TO OUR OWN RESEARCH ON THE PERIOD, WE FOUND THAT IN 1257, DARIM IBN-LA'AHAD, THE SON OF ALTAIR, OFFERED AN APPLE OF EDEN TO THE NEW SULTAN, WHICH SEEMINGLY STRENGTHENED HIS POWER.
ALL OF THE DATA HAS BEEN WRITTEN TO THIS DISC.
THIS OBJECT IS YOURS TOO.
STELLA WILL BE ABLE TO LEARN MORE ABOUT HER ANCESTOR, LUGOS, USING THIS OBJECT.
USE THIS INFORMATION AS BEST YOU CAN, HAWK. AND PLEASE INFORM MS. CROW THAT THE BROTHERHOOD OF ASSASSINS IS NOT THE PLACE TO START A *PISSING* CONTEST BETWEEN ITS MEMBERS.
IT HAS NEVER BEEN THE SUCCESS OF THE INDIVIDUAL THAT COUNTS, BUT THE ACCOMPLISHMENT OF OUR GOALS AS A TEAM.
I'LL, UH, REMEMBER TO PASS ON YOUR MESSAGE...
RIGHT--GOTTA GO. GOOD LUCK, AND I'LL SEE YA AROUND!
THANKS, JONATHAN.
GOOD LUCK, HAWK.
CAIRO. THE NEXT DAY.

15

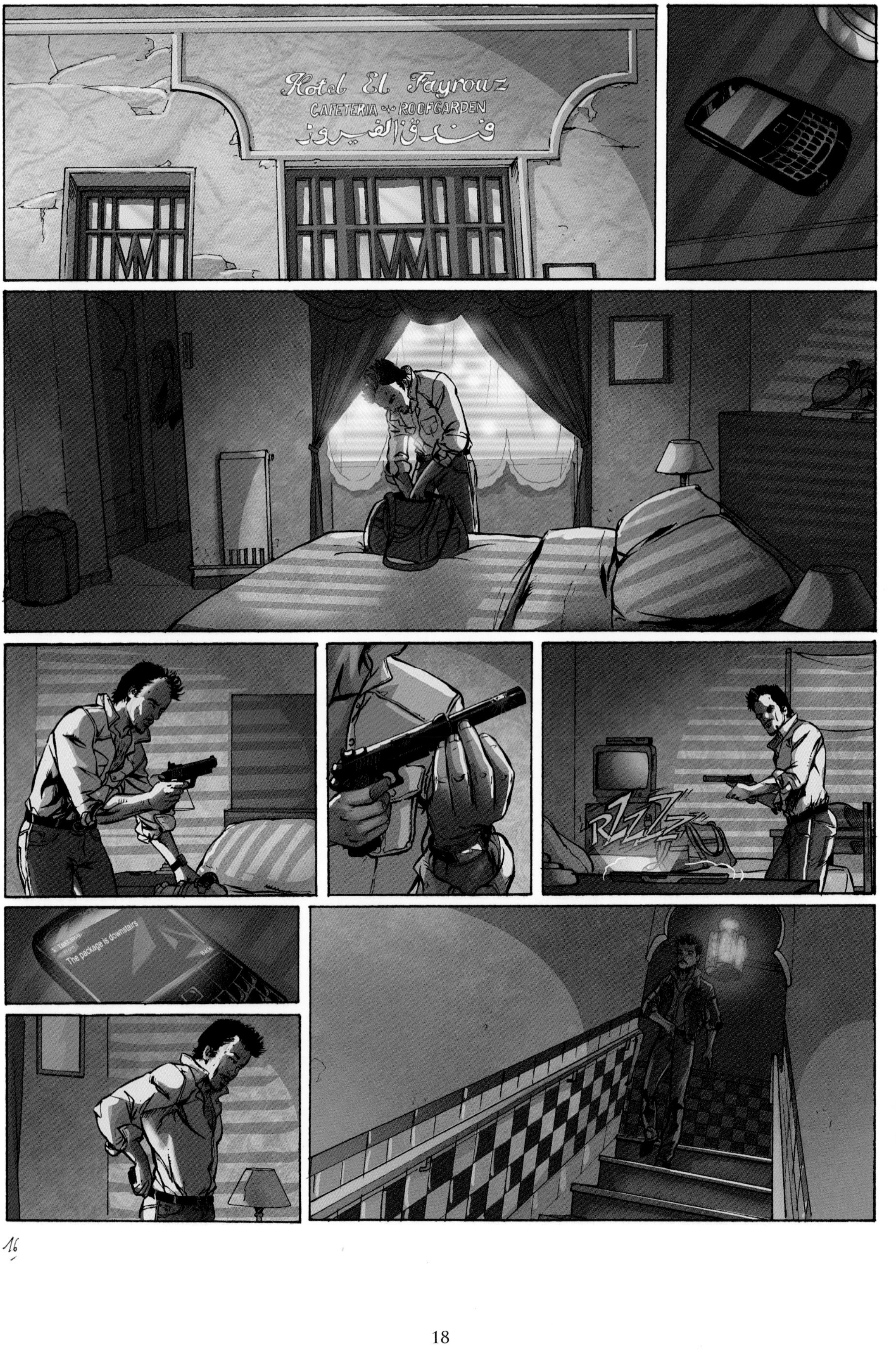
Hotel El Fayrouz
CAFETERIA ROOFGARDEN
فندق الفيروز
RZZZZ
The package is downstairs

16

VERNON HEST. PLEASED TO MEET YOU.

THE PLEASURE IS ALL MINE.

I'M SURPRISED, MR. HEST...

I THOUGHT THAT A MAN CAPABLE OF SPENDING SUCH A LARGE SUM IN ORDER TO GET WHATEVER HE WANTS WOULD HAVE THE MEANS TO OFFER A HOTEL WITH A TOUCH MORE... CLASS.

DO YOU HAVE IT?

OF COURSE.

HERE YOU GO.

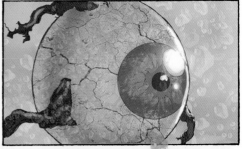

17

19

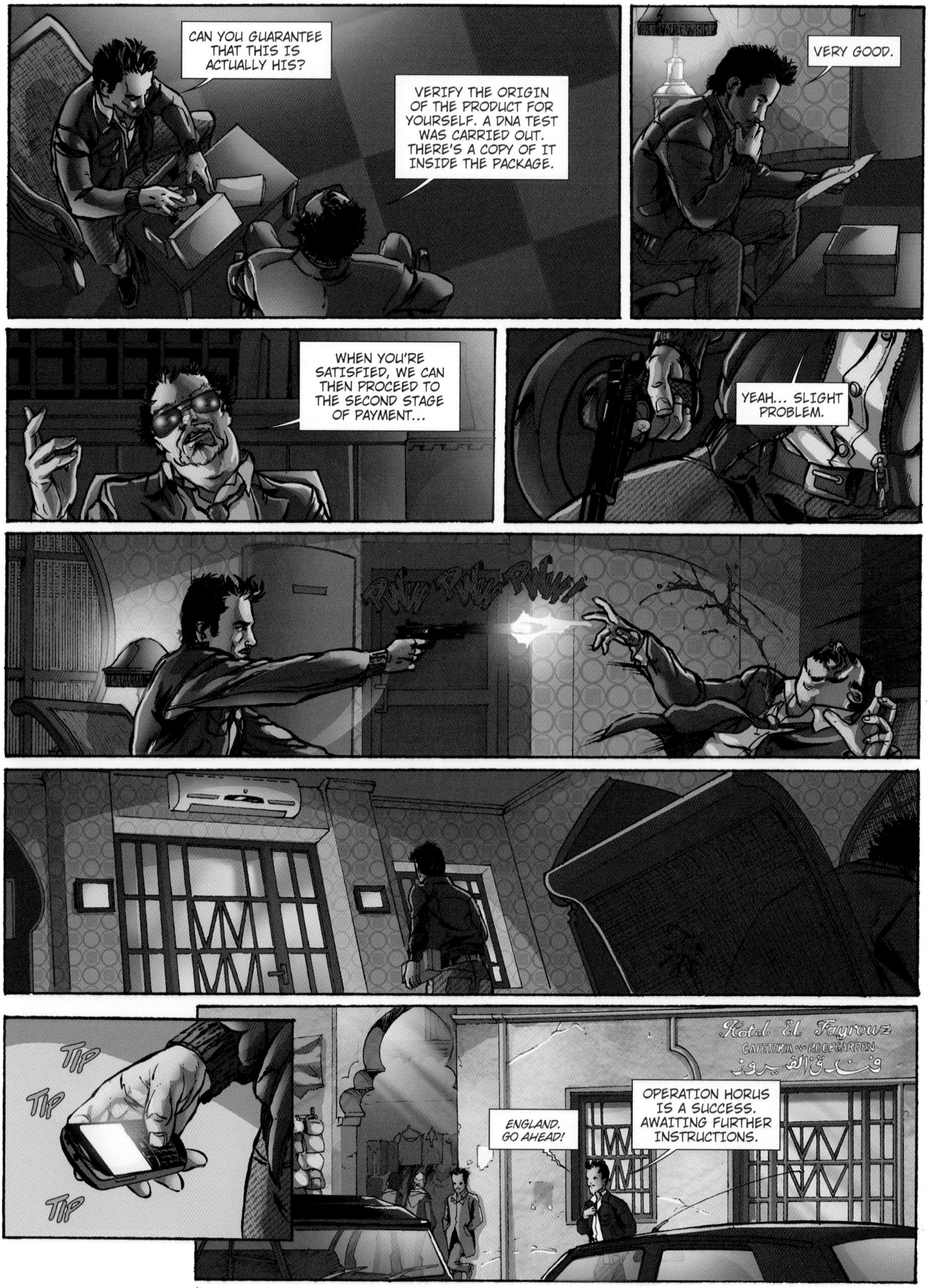
CAN YOU GUARANTEE THAT THIS IS ACTUALLY HIS?
VERIFY THE ORIGIN OF THE PRODUCT FOR YOURSELF. A DNA TEST WAS CARRIED OUT. THERE'S A COPY OF IT INSIDE THE PACKAGE.
VERY GOOD.
WHEN YOU'RE SATISFIED, WE CAN THEN PROCEED TO THE SECOND STAGE OF PAYMENT...
YEAH... SLIGHT PROBLEM.
TIP
TIP
TIP
Hotel El Fayrouz
CAFETERIA ROOFGARDEN
فندق الفيروز
ENGLAND. GO AHEAD!
OPERATION HORUS IS A SUCCESS. AWAITING FURTHER INSTRUCTIONS.

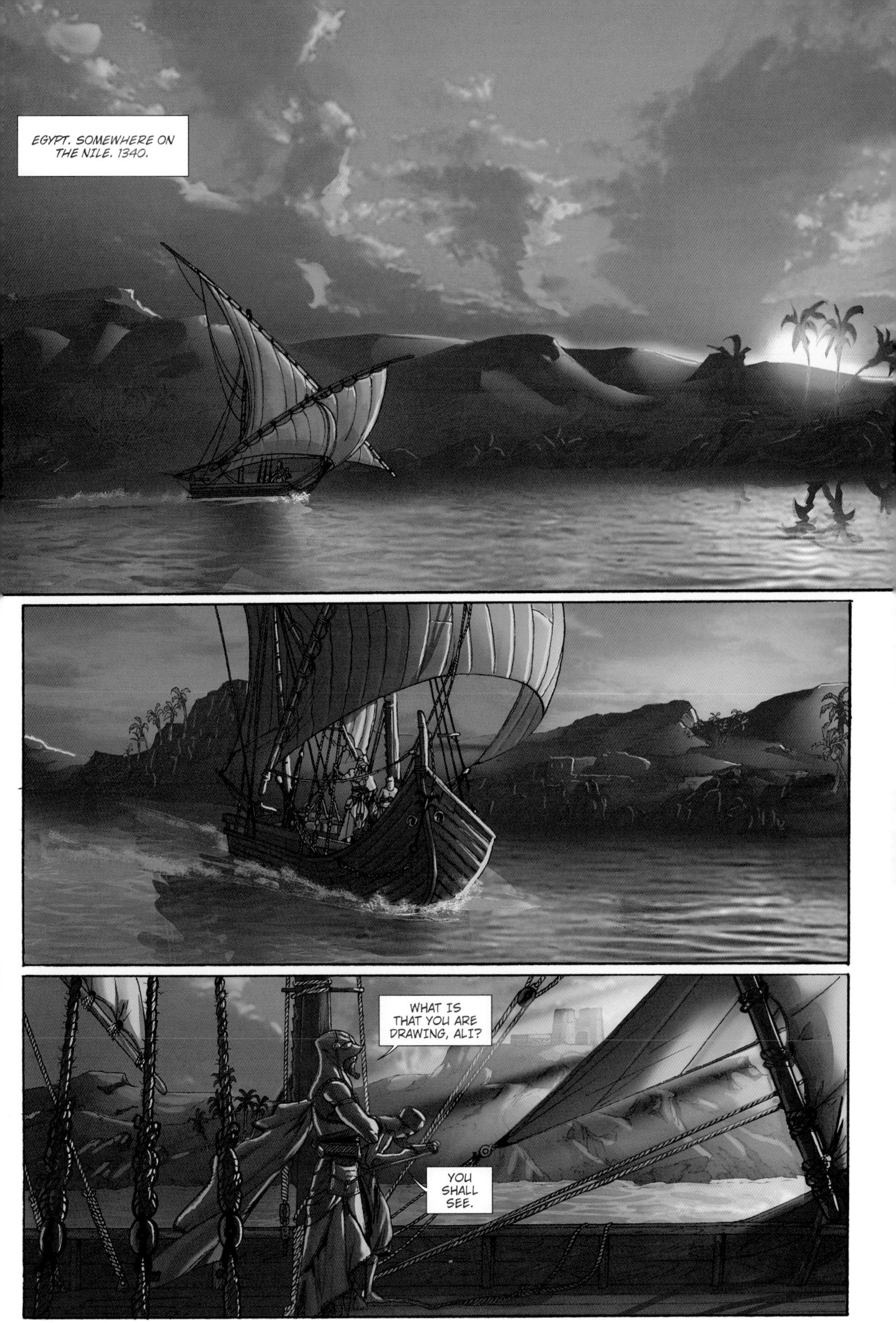
EGYPT. SOMEWHERE ON THE NILE. 1340.
WHAT IS THAT YOU ARE DRAWING, ALI?
YOU SHALL SEE.

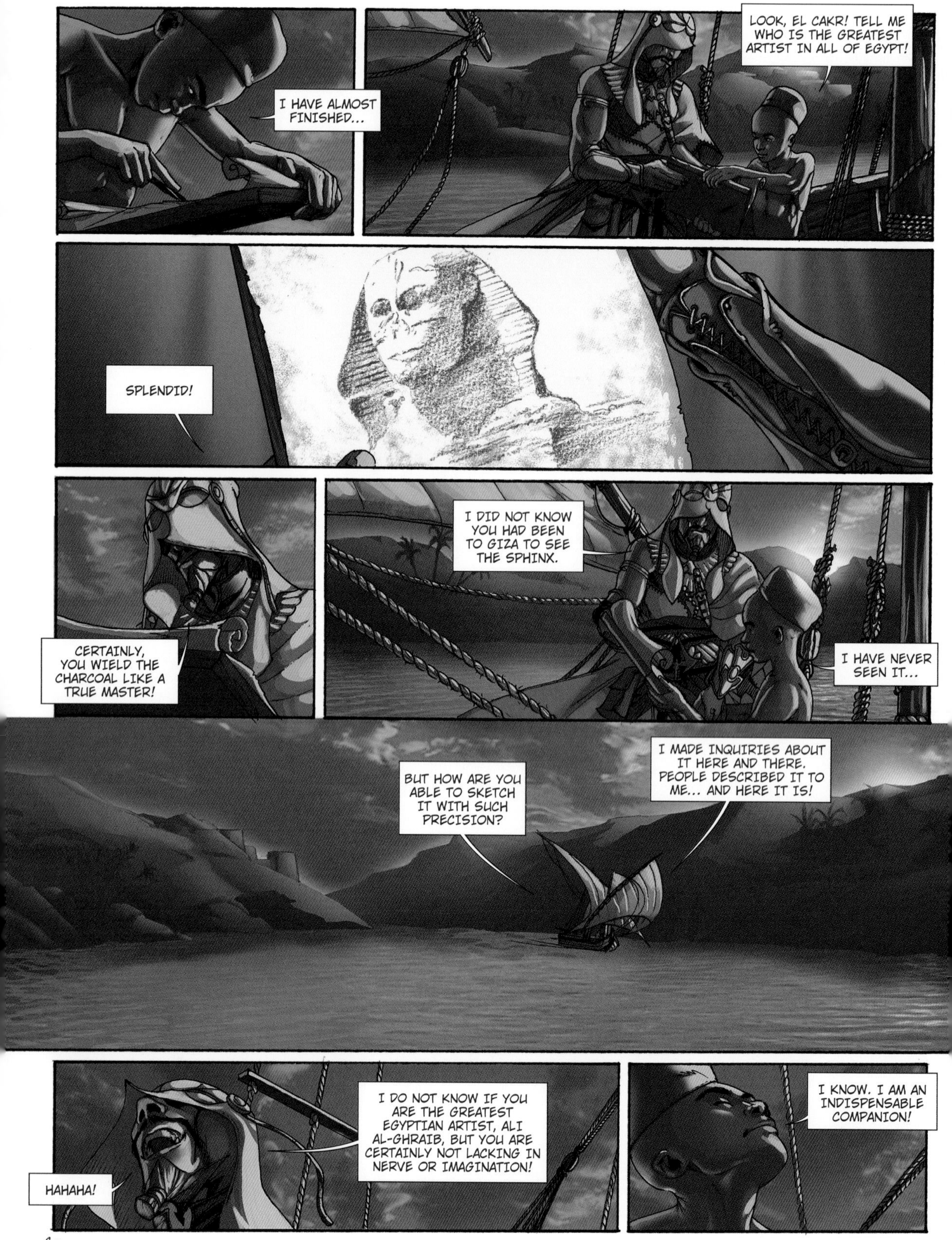
I HAVE ALMOST FINISHED...
LOOK, EL CAKR! TELL ME WHO IS THE GREATEST ARTIST IN ALL OF EGYPT!
SPLENDID!
CERTAINLY, YOU WIELD THE CHARCOAL LIKE A TRUE MASTER!
I DID NOT KNOW YOU HAD BEEN TO GIZA TO SEE THE SPHINX.
I HAVE NEVER SEEN IT...
BUT HOW ARE YOU ABLE TO SKETCH IT WITH SUCH PRECISION?
I MADE INQUIRIES ABOUT IT HERE AND THERE. PEOPLE DESCRIBED IT TO ME... AND HERE IT IS!
HAHAHA!
I DO NOT KNOW IF YOU ARE THE GREATEST EGYPTIAN ARTIST, ALI AL-GHRAIB, BUT YOU ARE CERTAINLY NOT LACKING IN NERVE OR IMAGINATION!
I KNOW. I AM AN INDISPENSABLE COMPANION!
20

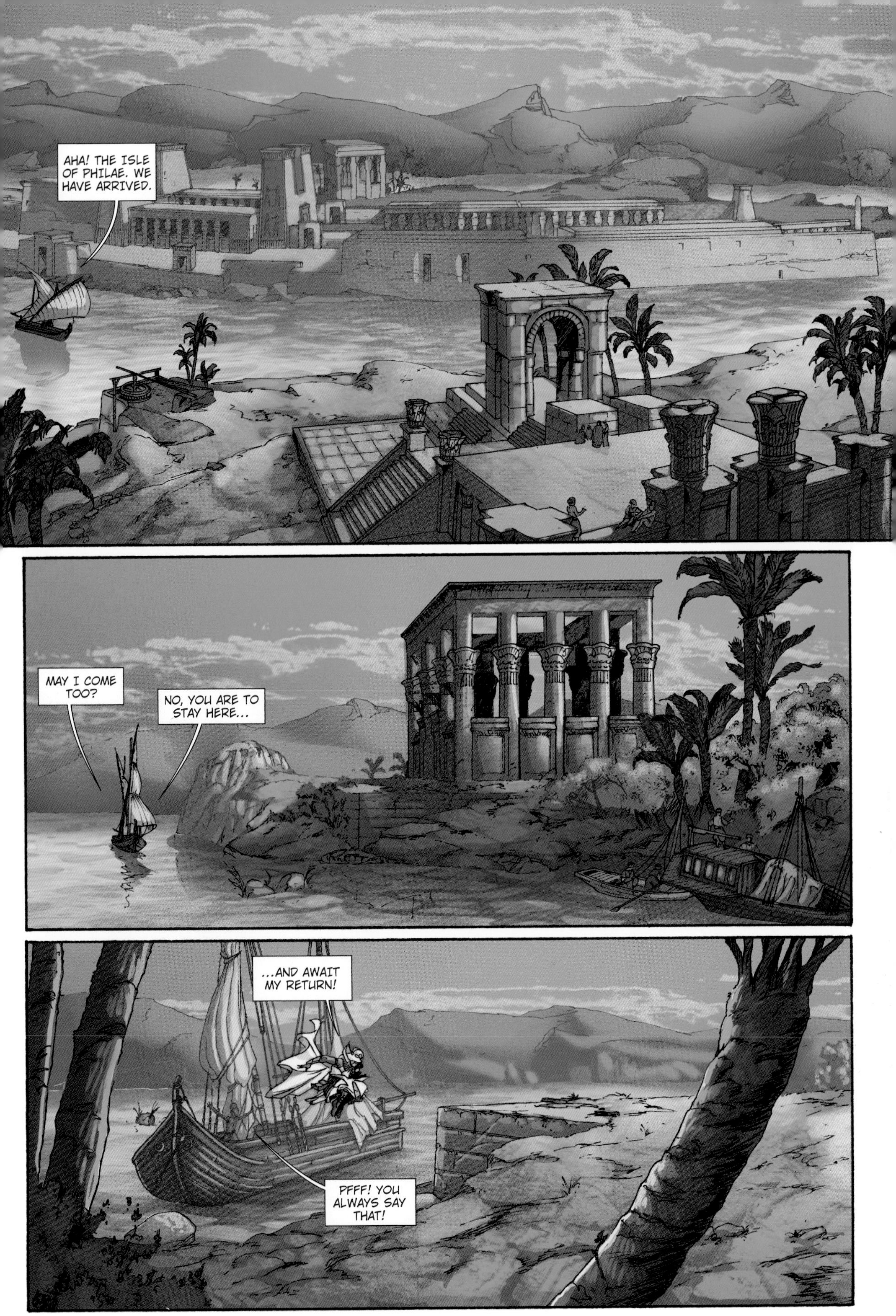
AHA! THE ISLE OF PHILAE. WE HAVE ARRIVED.
MAY I COME TOO?
NO, YOU ARE TO STAY HERE...
...AND AWAIT MY RETURN!
PFFF! YOU ALWAYS SAY THAT!

21

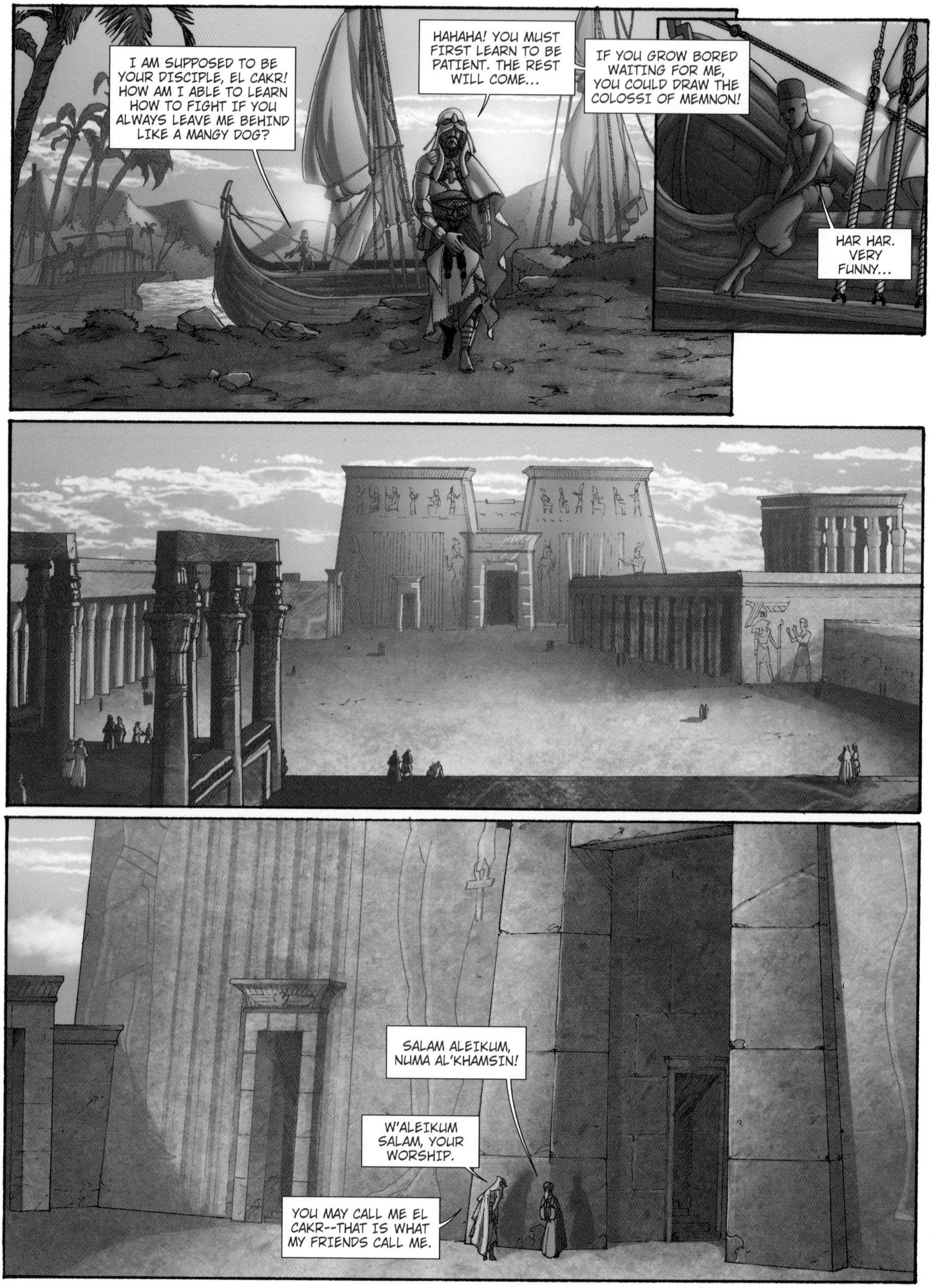
I AM SUPPOSED TO BE YOUR DISCIPLE, EL CAKR! HOW AM I ABLE TO LEARN HOW TO FIGHT IF YOU ALWAYS LEAVE ME BEHIND LIKE A MANGY DOG?
HAHAHA! YOU MUST FIRST LEARN TO BE PATIENT. THE REST WILL COME...
IF YOU GROW BORED WAITING FOR ME, YOU COULD DRAW THE COLOSSI OF MEMNON!
HAR HAR. VERY FUNNY...
SALAM ALEIKUM, NUMA AL'KHAMSIN!
W'ALEIKUM SALAM, YOUR WORSHIP.
YOU MAY CALL ME EL CAKR--THAT IS WHAT MY FRIENDS CALL ME.

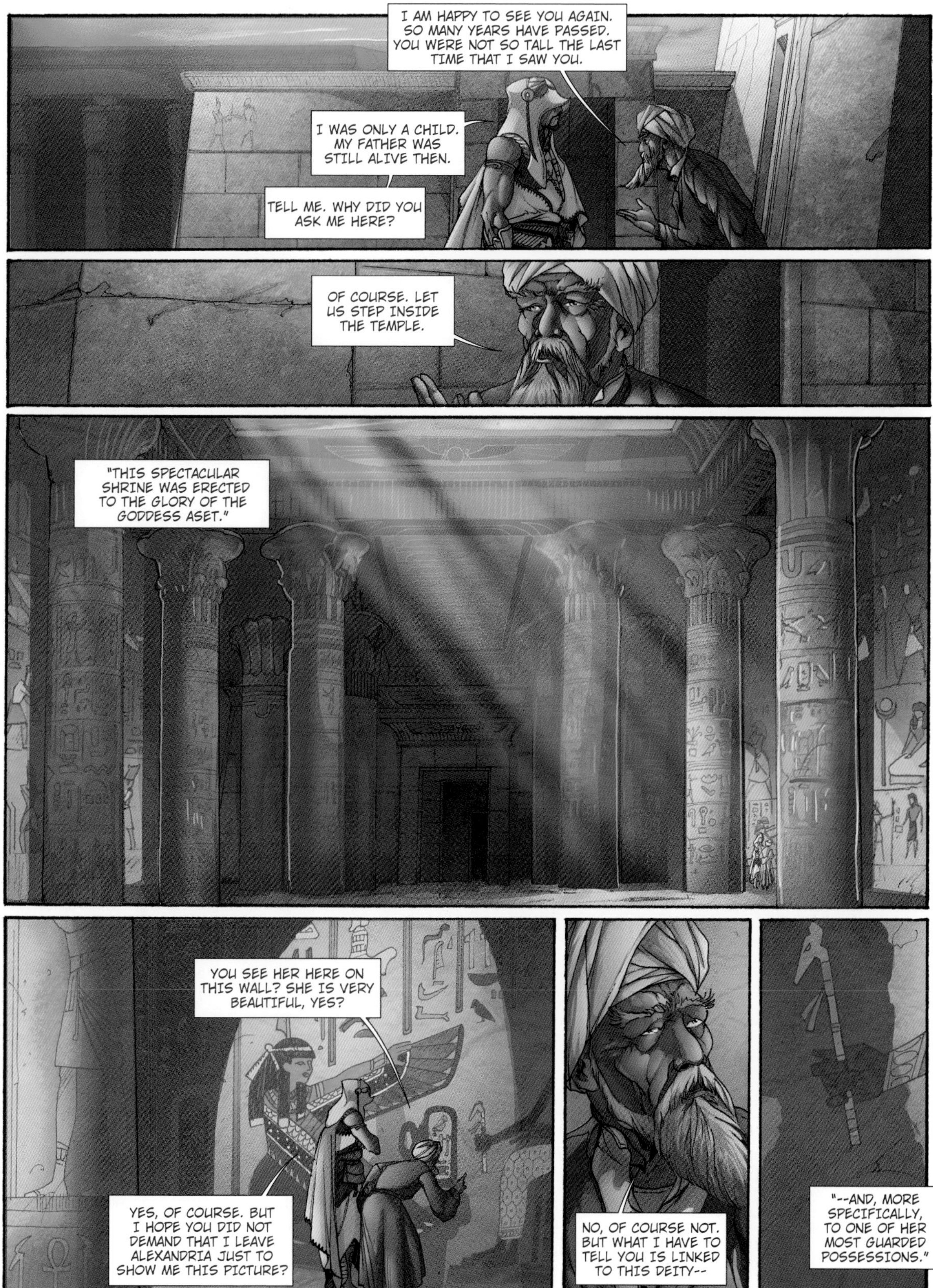
I AM HAPPY TO SEE YOU AGAIN. SO MANY YEARS HAVE PASSED. YOU WERE NOT SO TALL THE LAST TIME THAT I SAW YOU.
I WAS ONLY A CHILD. MY FATHER WAS STILL ALIVE THEN.
TELL ME. WHY DID YOU ASK ME HERE?
OF COURSE. LET US STEP INSIDE THE TEMPLE.
"THIS SPECTACULAR SHRINE WAS ERECTED TO THE GLORY OF THE GODDESS ASET."
YOU SEE HER HERE ON THIS WALL? SHE IS VERY BEAUTIFUL, YES?
YES, OF COURSE. BUT I HOPE YOU DID NOT DEMAND THAT I LEAVE ALEXANDRIA JUST TO SHOW ME THIS PICTURE?
NO, OF COURSE NOT. BUT WHAT I HAVE TO TELL YOU IS LINKED TO THIS DEITY--
"--AND, MORE SPECIFICALLY, TO ONE OF HER MOST GUARDED POSSESSIONS."

23

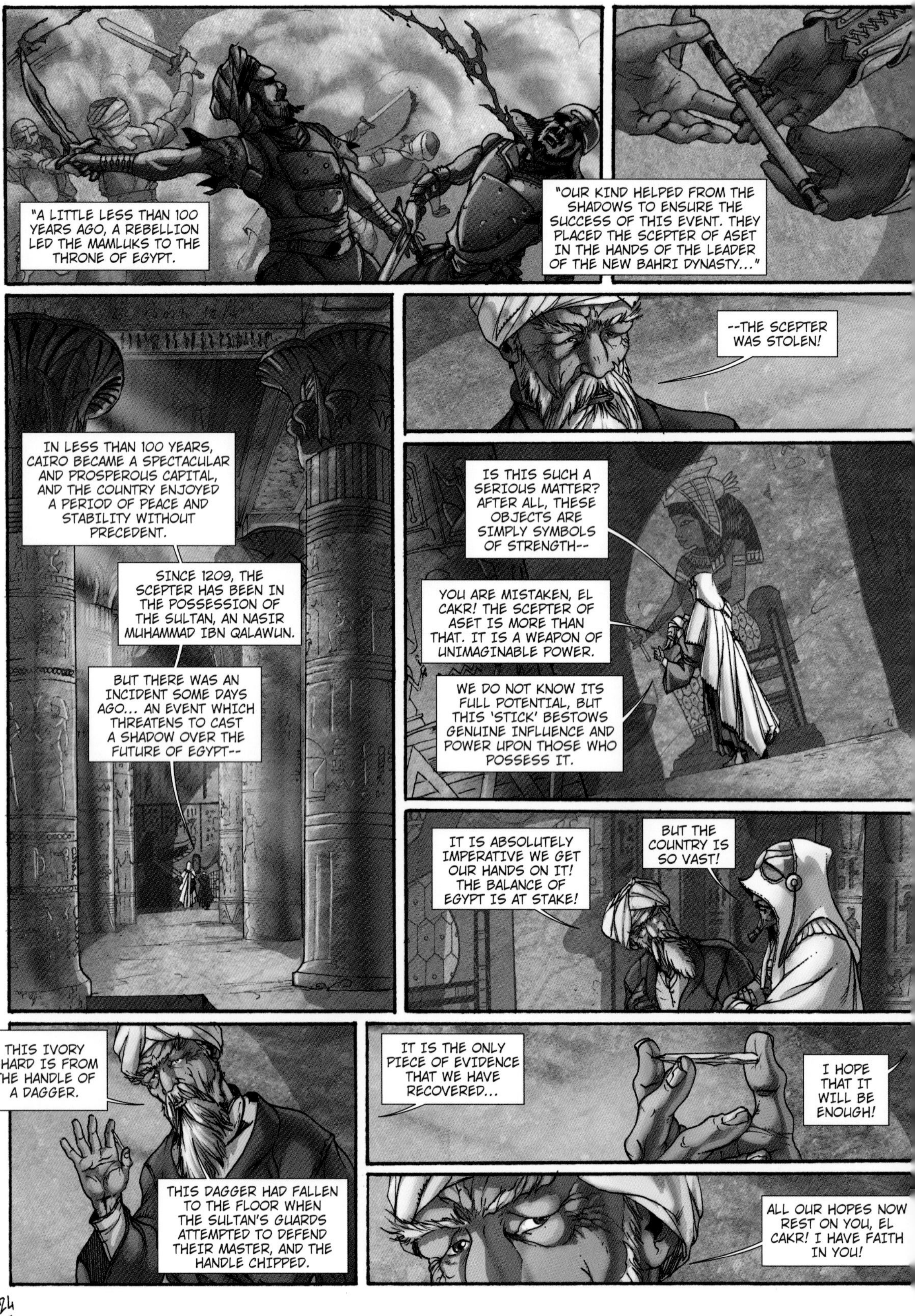
"A LITTLE LESS THAN 100 YEARS AGO, A REBELLION LED THE MAMLUKS TO THE THRONE OF EGYPT.
"OUR KIND HELPED FROM THE SHADOWS TO ENSURE THE SUCCESS OF THIS EVENT. THEY PLACED THE SCEPTER OF ASET IN THE HANDS OF THE LEADER OF THE NEW BAHRI DYNASTY..."
IN LESS THAN 100 YEARS, CAIRO BECAME A SPECTACULAR AND PROSPEROUS CAPITAL, AND THE COUNTRY ENJOYED A PERIOD OF PEACE AND STABILITY WITHOUT PRECEDENT.
SINCE 1209, THE SCEPTER HAS BEEN IN THE POSSESSION OF THE SULTAN, AN NASIR MUHAMMAD IBN QALAWUN.
BUT THERE WAS AN INCIDENT SOME DAYS AGO... AN EVENT WHICH THREATENS TO CAST A SHADOW OVER THE FUTURE OF EGYPT--
--THE SCEPTER WAS STOLEN!
IS THIS SUCH A SERIOUS MATTER? AFTER ALL, THESE OBJECTS ARE SIMPLY SYMBOLS OF STRENGTH--
YOU ARE MISTAKEN, EL CAKR! THE SCEPTER OF ASET IS MORE THAN THAT. IT IS A WEAPON OF UNIMAGINABLE POWER.
WE DO NOT KNOW ITS FULL POTENTIAL, BUT THIS 'STICK' BESTOWS GENUINE INFLUENCE AND POWER UPON THOSE WHO POSSESS IT.
IT IS ABSOLUTELY IMPERATIVE WE GET OUR HANDS ON IT! THE BALANCE OF EGYPT IS AT STAKE!
BUT THE COUNTRY IS SO VAST!
THIS IVORY SHARD IS FROM THE HANDLE OF A DAGGER.
THIS DAGGER HAD FALLEN TO THE FLOOR WHEN THE SULTAN'S GUARDS ATTEMPTED TO DEFEND THEIR MASTER, AND THE HANDLE CHIPPED.
IT IS THE ONLY PIECE OF EVIDENCE THAT WE HAVE RECOVERED...
I HOPE THAT IT WILL BE ENOUGH!
ALL OUR HOPES NOW REST ON YOU, EL CAKR! I HAVE FAITH IN YOU!
24

AAAHHH!

WHAT'S HAPPENING, STELLA?

WE DON'T KNOW! EVERYTHING WAS FINE! NANCY PROGRAMMED THE TIME ON THE ANIMUS ACCORDING TO THE SPECIFIC FEATURES OF HIS PROFILE... HE'S NOWHERE NEAR THE LIMIT OF RISK!

GOD, I HOPE HE HASN'T SUFFERED A STROKE!

HE'S NOT REGAINING CONSCIOUSNESS!

PREPARE THE MED TEAM! HE NEEDS TO BE TAKEN TO THE INFIRMARY RIGHT NOW!

OKAY, OKAY, I'M CALLING THEM!

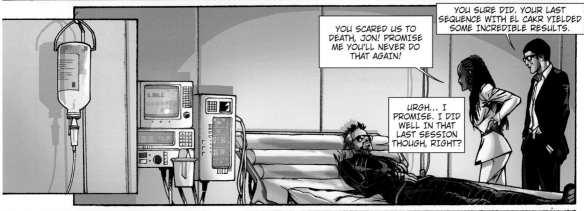

YOU SCARED US TO DEATH, JON! PROMISE ME YOU'LL NEVER DO THAT AGAIN!

YOU SURE DID. YOUR LAST SEQUENCE WITH EL CAKR YIELDED SOME INCREDIBLE RESULTS.

URGH... I PROMISE. I DID WELL IN THAT LAST SESSION THOUGH, RIGHT?

WE NOW HAVE A BETTER UNDERSTANDING OF THE SCEPTER'S IMPORTANCE, AND WHY LUGOS FOUNDED THE 'LIBERALIS CIRCULUM' AROUND THE OBJECT!

WE NEED TO DRAW UP A REPORT AND SEND IT TO ALL THE CELLS. THEY NEED TO BE INFORMED OF THIS DISCOVERY AND ITS INCREDIBLE VALUE. ALL OF OUR RESOURCES NEED TO BE MOBILISED AND FOCUSED ON FINDING THIS ARTIFACT.

I'LL TAKE CARE OF IT RIGHT AWAY.

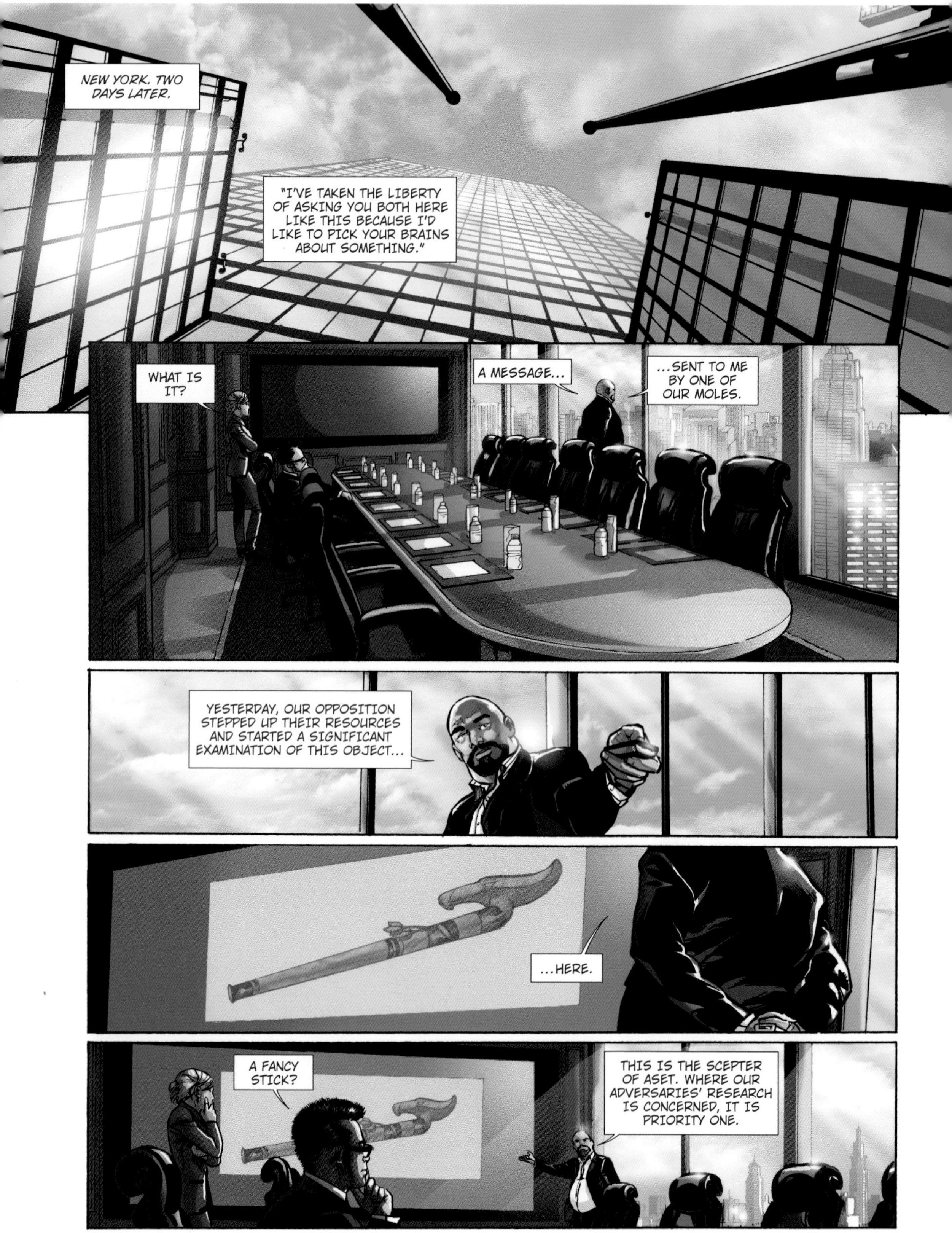
NEW YORK. TWO DAYS LATER.
"I'VE TAKEN THE LIBERTY OF ASKING YOU BOTH HERE LIKE THIS BECAUSE I'D LIKE TO PICK YOUR BRAINS ABOUT SOMETHING."
WHAT IS IT?
A MESSAGE...
...SENT TO ME BY ONE OF OUR MOLES.
YESTERDAY, OUR OPPOSITION STEPPED UP THEIR RESOURCES AND STARTED A SIGNIFICANT EXAMINATION OF THIS OBJECT...
...HERE.
A FANCY STICK?
THIS IS THE SCEPTER OF ASET. WHERE OUR ADVERSARIES' RESEARCH IS CONCERNED, IT IS PRIORITY ONE.

"THIS OBJECT IS ONE OF THE MOST VALUABLE ITEMS SOUGHT BY OUR ORDER!

"IT IS INVALUABLE TO OUR CAUSE. IT WOULD GIVE US UNBELIEVABLE POWER, AND WOULD GUARANTEE THE ORDER VICTORY OVER ITS ENEMIES!"

MY QUESTION IS SIMPLE: WHAT DO YOU THINK?

THIS IS A TRAP. AND AN UNSOPHISTICATED ONE AT THAT!

IT'S A LURE--THEY'RE SHAKING THIS ARTIFACT UNDER OUR NOSES. THEY WANT TO FORCE US TO TAKE PREMATURE ACTION.

IF WE REACT, WE'LL GET FOUND OUT. AND OUR AGENTS' COVERS WILL BE *BLOWN* ALONG THE WAY!

ALL I'M SAYING IS, WE NEED TO BE *EXTREMELY* CAREFUL.

UNDERSTOOD.

LAETICIA?

I THINK THE OPPOSITE-- WE SHOULD TAKE THIS INFORMATION SERIOUSLY AND ACT AS QUICKLY AS POSSIBLE.

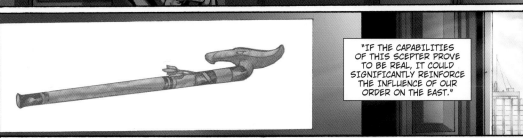

"IF THE CAPABILITIES OF THIS SCEPTER PROVE TO BE REAL, IT COULD SIGNIFICANTLY REINFORCE THE INFLUENCE OF OUR ORDER ON THE EAST."

THANK YOU BOTH. I WILL TAKE YOUR COMMENTS ON BOARD...

I'M GOING TO PLACE ONE OF OUR MOST CAREFUL AND EFFECTIVE FIELD AGENTS IN THIS MISSION.

"LAETICIA, I'D LIKE YOU TO MAKE CONTACT WITH VERNON HEST TODAY."

"UNDERSTOOD, MR. RIKKIN."

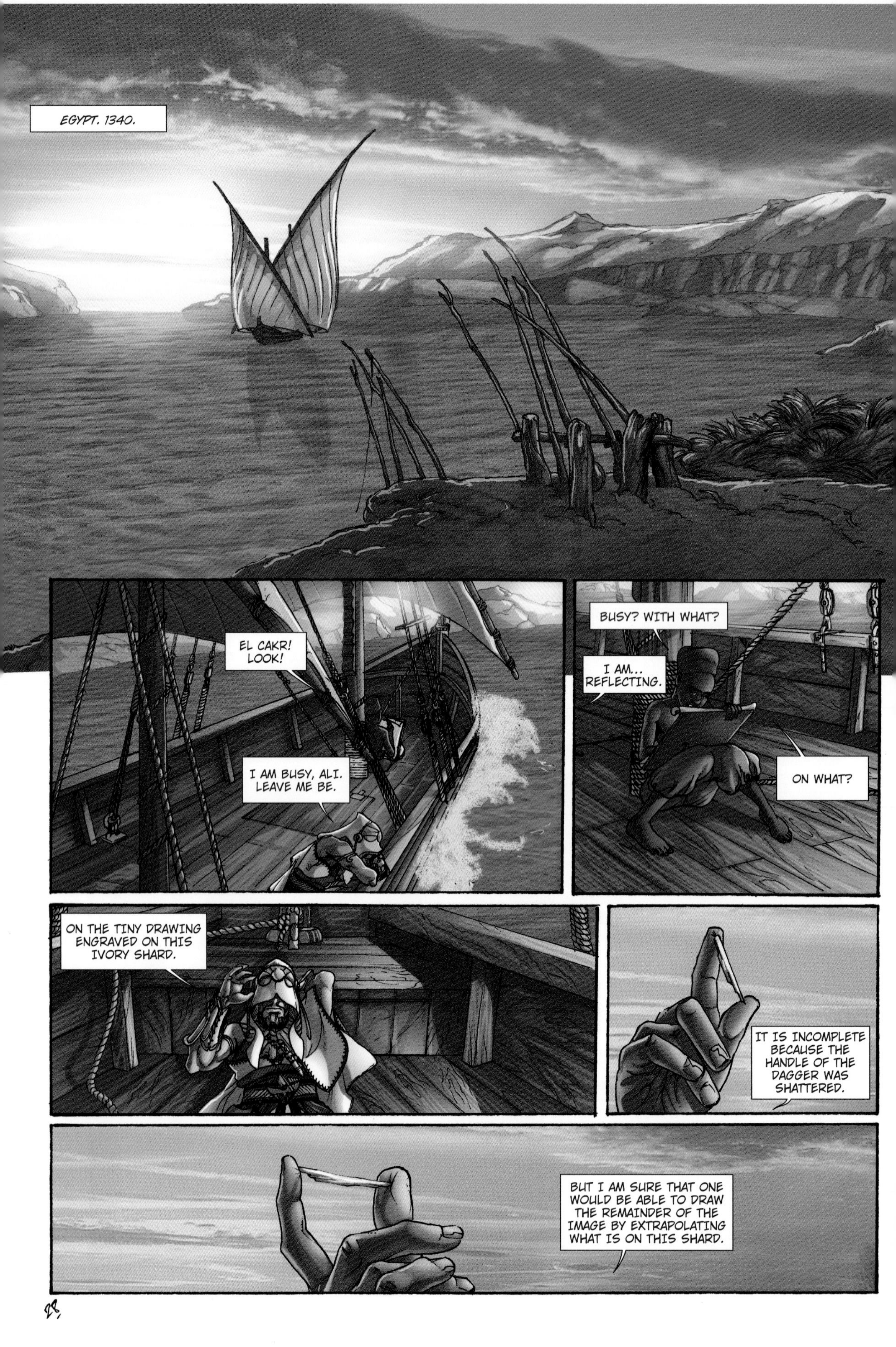
EGYPT. 1340.
EL CAKR! LOOK!
I AM BUSY, ALI. LEAVE ME BE.
BUSY? WITH WHAT?
I AM... REFLECTING.
ON WHAT?
ON THE TINY DRAWING ENGRAVED ON THIS IVORY SHARD.
IT IS INCOMPLETE BECAUSE THE HANDLE OF THE DAGGER WAS SHATTERED.
BUT I AM SURE THAT ONE WOULD BE ABLE TO DRAW THE REMAINDER OF THE IMAGE BY EXTRAPOLATING WHAT IS ON THIS SHARD.

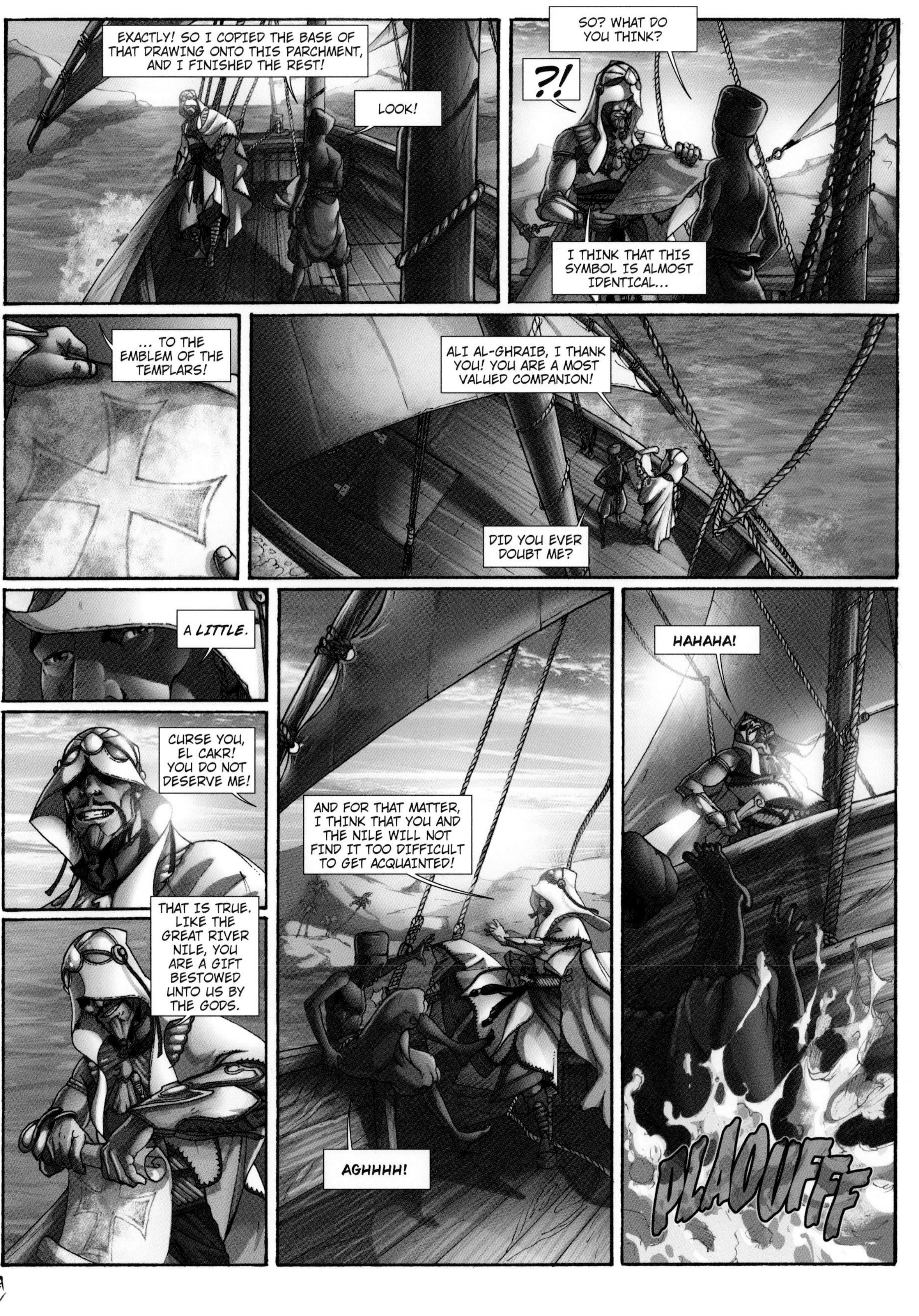
EXACTLY! SO I COPIED THE BASE OF THAT DRAWING ONTO THIS PARCHMENT, AND I FINISHED THE REST!
LOOK!
SO? WHAT DO YOU THINK?
?!
I THINK THAT THIS SYMBOL IS ALMOST IDENTICAL...
... TO THE EMBLEM OF THE TEMPLARS!
ALI AL-GHRAIB, I THANK YOU! YOU ARE A MOST VALUED COMPANION!
DID YOU EVER DOUBT ME?
A LITTLE.
CURSE YOU, EL CAKR! YOU DO NOT DESERVE ME!
THAT IS TRUE. LIKE THE GREAT RIVER NILE, YOU ARE A GIFT BESTOWED UNTO US BY THE GODS.
AND FOR THAT MATTER, I THINK THAT YOU AND THE NILE WILL NOT FIND IT TOO DIFFICULT TO GET ACQUAINTED!
AGHHHH!
HAHAHA!
PLAOUFFF

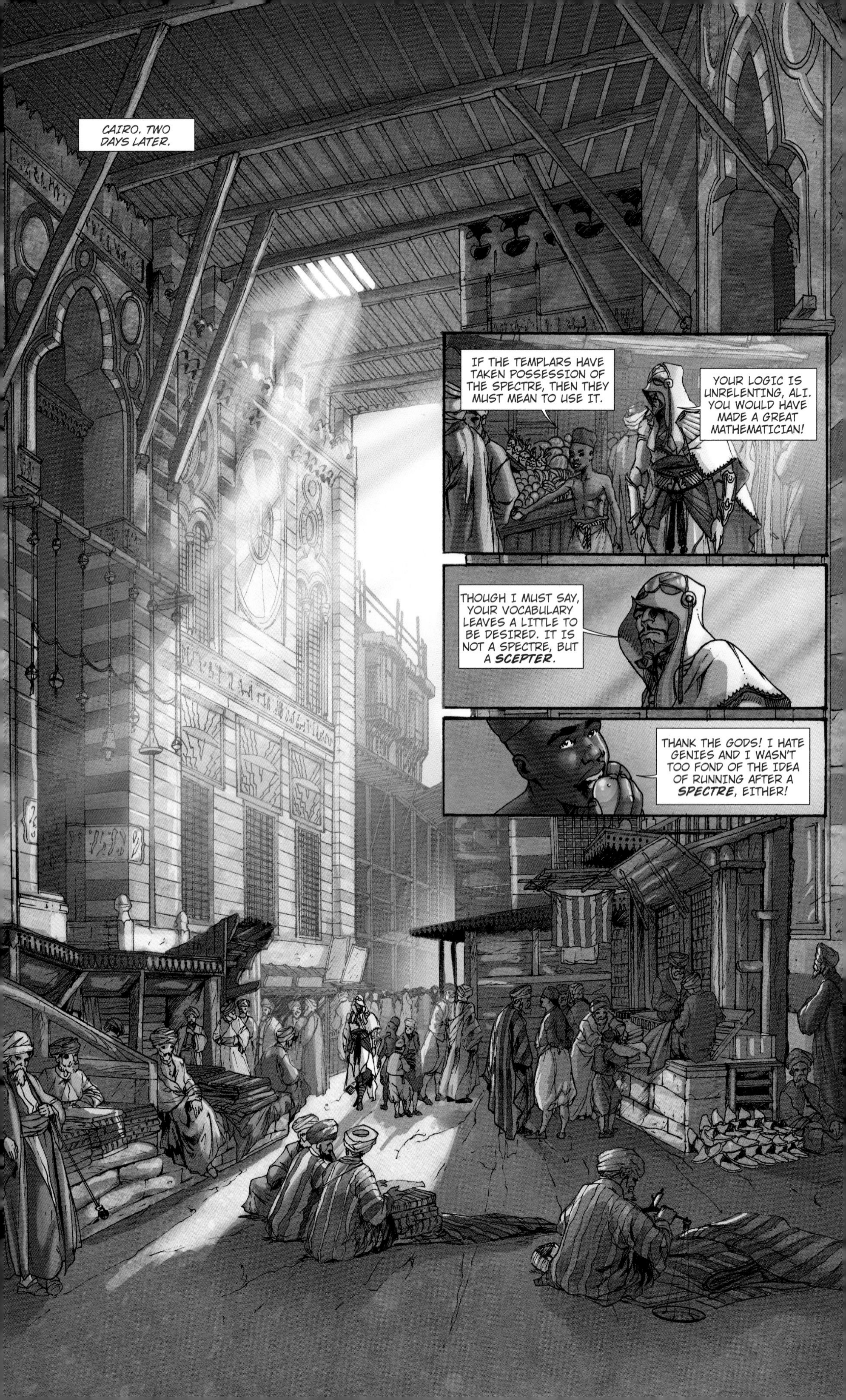
CAIRO. TWO DAYS LATER.
IF THE TEMPLARS HAVE TAKEN POSSESSION OF THE SPECTRE, THEN THEY MUST MEAN TO USE IT.
YOUR LOGIC IS UNRELENTING, ALI. YOU WOULD HAVE MADE A GREAT MATHEMATICIAN!
THOUGH I MUST SAY, YOUR VOCABULARY LEAVES A LITTLE TO BE DESIRED. IT IS NOT A SPECTRE, BUT A ***SCEPTER***.
THANK THE GODS! I HATE GENIES AND I WASN'T TOO FOND OF THE IDEA OF RUNNING AFTER A ***SPECTRE***, EITHER!

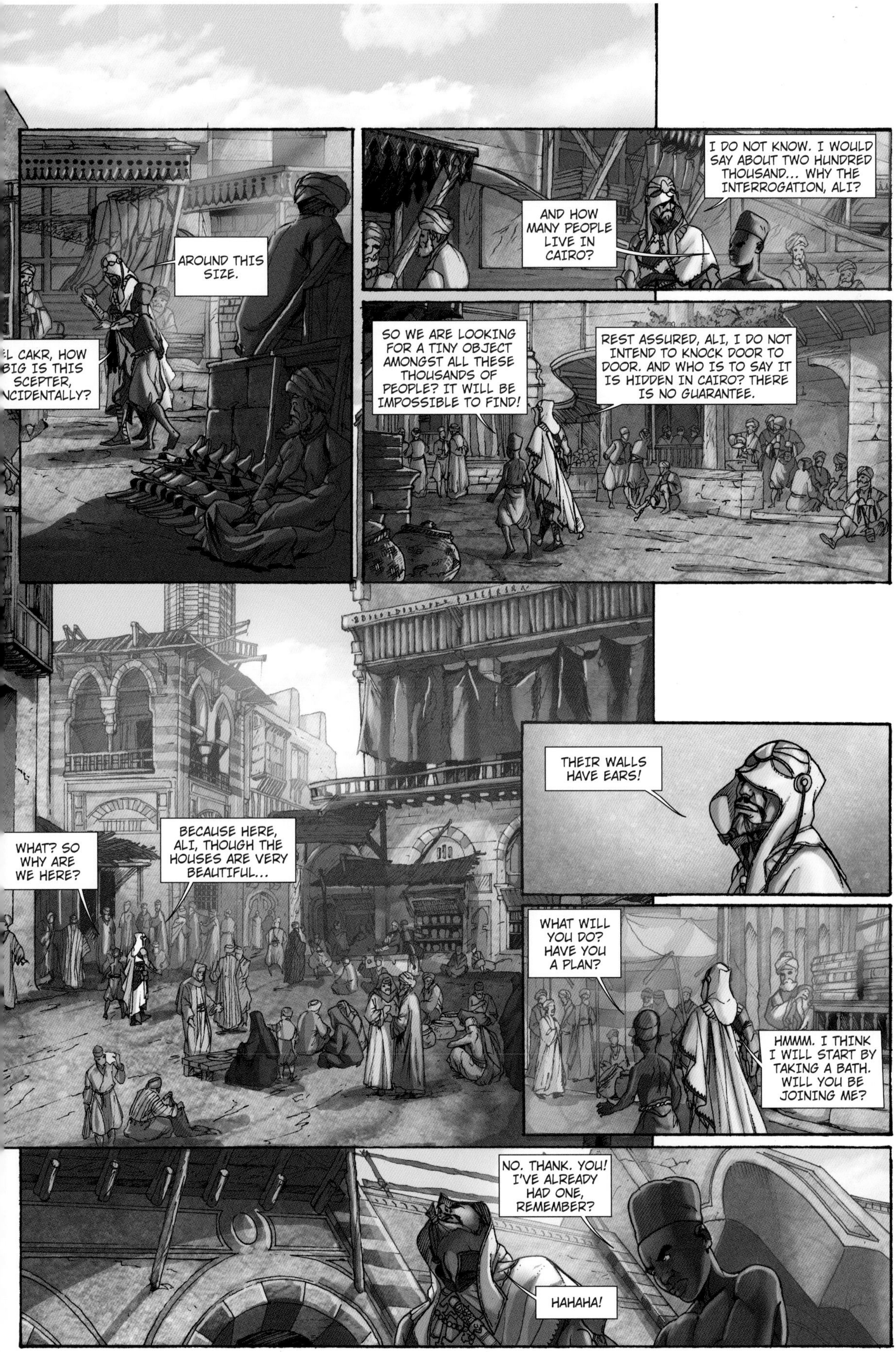

L CAKR, HOW BIG IS THIS SCEPTER, NCIDENTALLY?
AROUND THIS SIZE.
AND HOW MANY PEOPLE LIVE IN CAIRO?
I DO NOT KNOW. I WOULD SAY ABOUT TWO HUNDRED THOUSAND... WHY THE INTERROGATION, ALI?
SO WE ARE LOOKING FOR A TINY OBJECT AMONGST ALL THESE THOUSANDS OF PEOPLE? IT WILL BE IMPOSSIBLE TO FIND!
REST ASSURED, ALI, I DO NOT INTEND TO KNOCK DOOR TO DOOR. AND WHO IS TO SAY IT IS HIDDEN IN CAIRO? THERE IS NO GUARANTEE.
WHAT? SO WHY ARE WE HERE?
BECAUSE HERE, ALI, THOUGH THE HOUSES ARE VERY BEAUTIFUL...
THEIR WALLS HAVE EARS!
WHAT WILL YOU DO? HAVE YOU A PLAN?
HMMM. I THINK I WILL START BY TAKING A BATH. WILL YOU BE JOINING ME?
NO. THANK. YOU! I'VE ALREADY HAD ONE, REMEMBER?
HAHAHA!

31

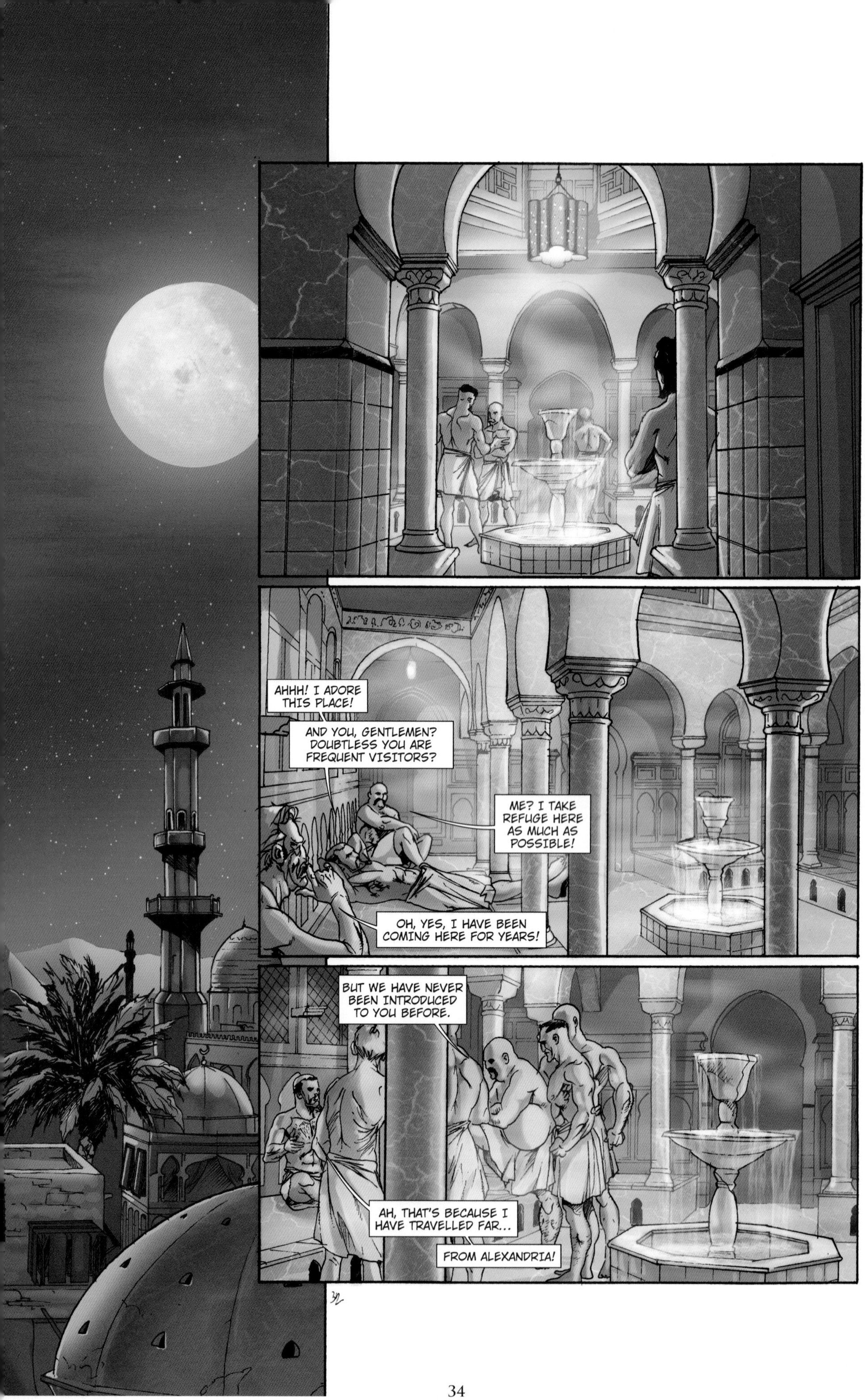
AHHH! I ADORE THIS PLACE!
AND YOU, GENTLEMEN? DOUBTLESS YOU ARE FREQUENT VISITORS?
ME? I TAKE REFUGE HERE AS MUCH AS POSSIBLE!
OH, YES, I HAVE BEEN COMING HERE FOR YEARS!
BUT WE HAVE NEVER BEEN INTRODUCED TO YOU BEFORE.
AH, THAT'S BECAUSE I HAVE TRAVELLED FAR...
FROM ALEXANDRIA!

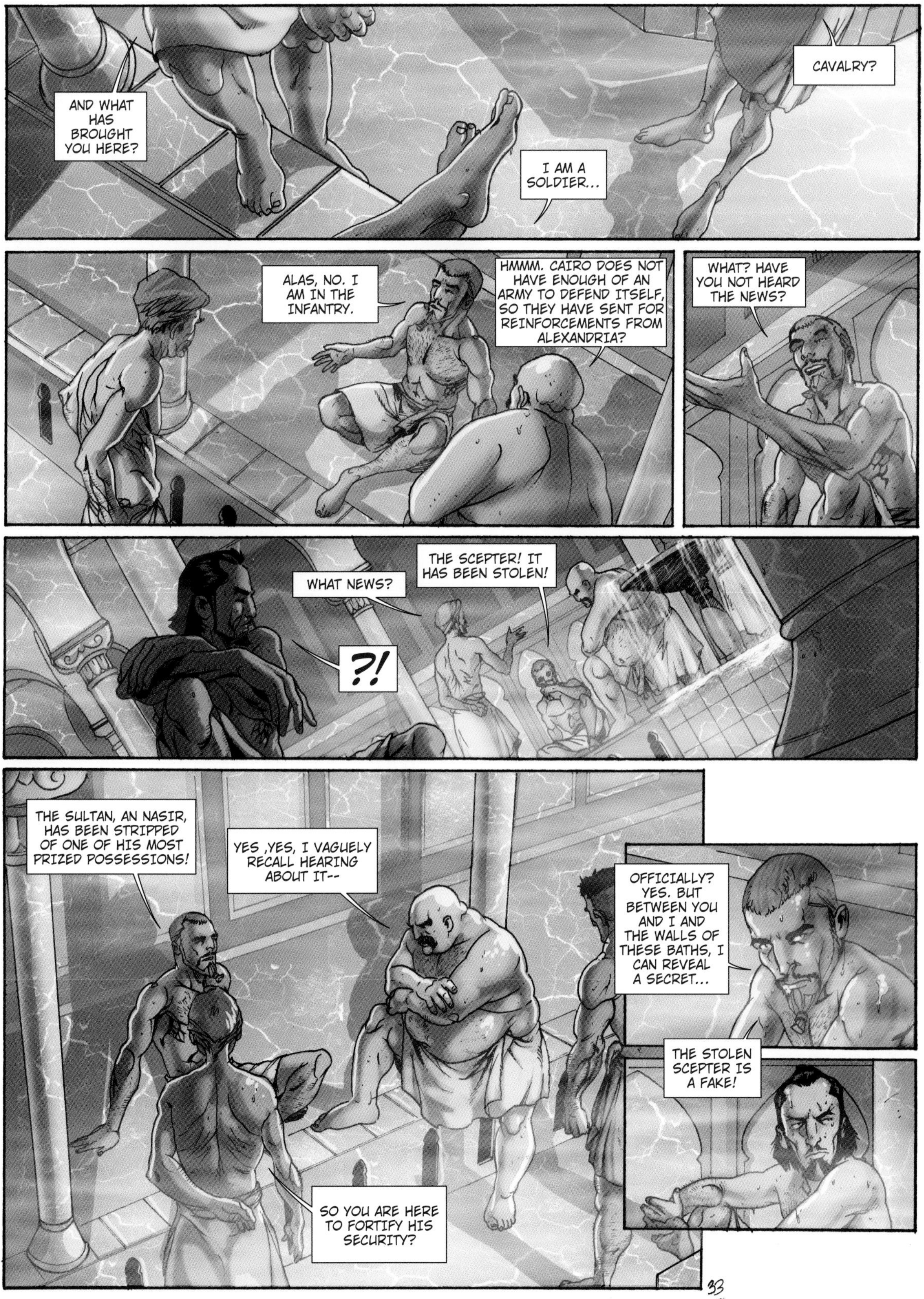
AND WHAT HAS BROUGHT YOU HERE?
I AM A SOLDIER...
CAVALRY?
ALAS, NO. I AM IN THE INFANTRY.
HMMM. CAIRO DOES NOT HAVE ENOUGH OF AN ARMY TO DEFEND ITSELF, SO THEY HAVE SENT FOR REINFORCEMENTS FROM ALEXANDRIA?
WHAT? HAVE YOU NOT HEARD THE NEWS?
WHAT NEWS?
?!
THE SCEPTER! IT HAS BEEN STOLEN!
THE SULTAN, AN NASIR, HAS BEEN STRIPPED OF ONE OF HIS MOST PRIZED POSSESSIONS!
YES ,YES, I VAGUELY RECALL HEARING ABOUT IT--
SO YOU ARE HERE TO FORTIFY HIS SECURITY?
OFFICIALLY? YES. BUT BETWEEN YOU AND I AND THE WALLS OF THESE BATHS, I CAN REVEAL A SECRET...
THE STOLEN SCEPTER IS A FAKE!
33

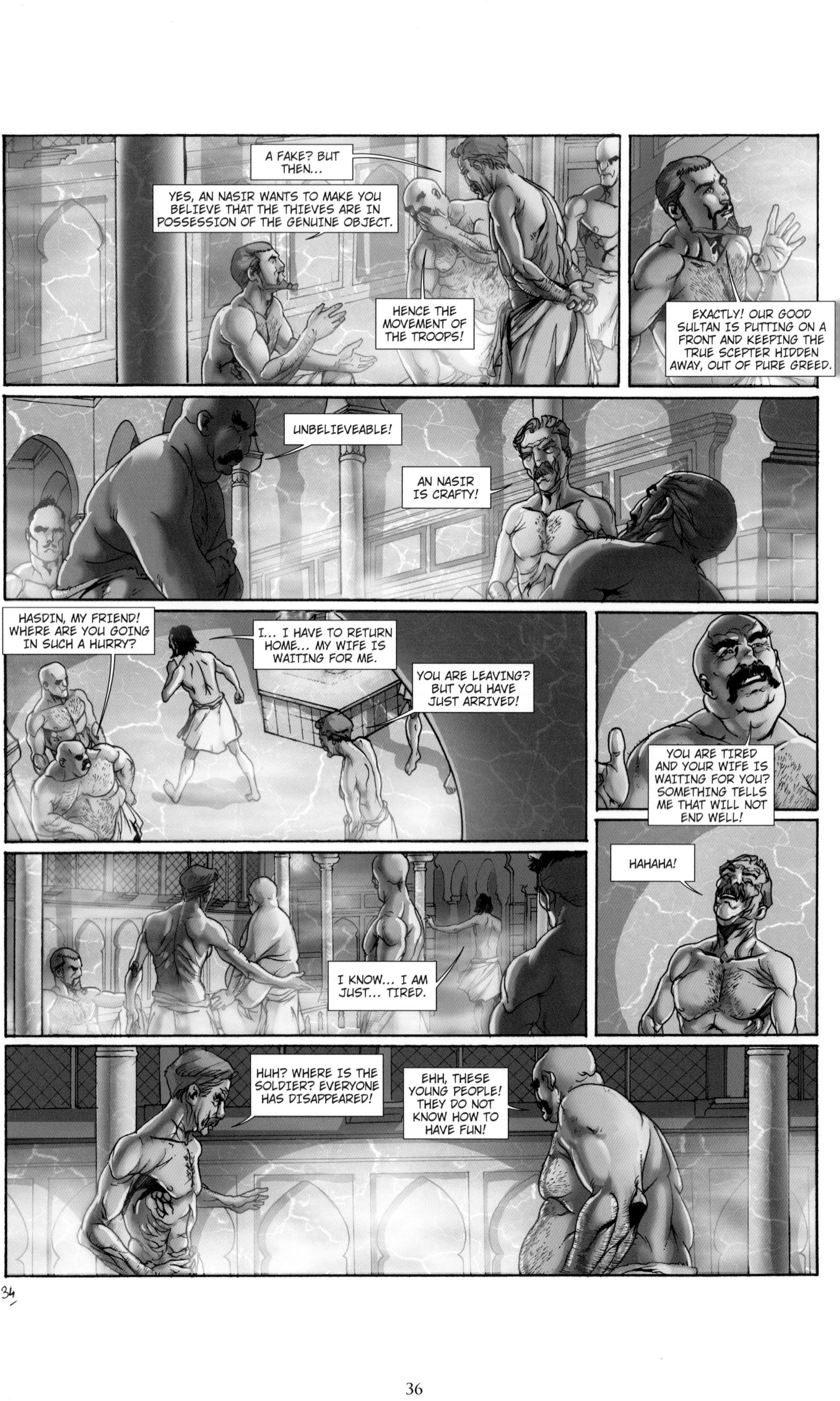

A FAKE? BUT THEN...
YES, AN NASIR WANTS TO MAKE YOU BELIEVE THAT THE THIEVES ARE IN POSSESSION OF THE GENUINE OBJECT.
HENCE THE MOVEMENT OF THE TROOPS!
EXACTLY! OUR GOOD SULTAN IS PUTTING ON A FRONT AND KEEPING THE TRUE SCEPTER HIDDEN AWAY, OUT OF PURE GREED.
UNBELIEVEABLE!
AN NASIR IS CRAFTY!
HASDIN, MY FRIEND! WHERE ARE YOU GOING IN SUCH A HURRY?
I... I HAVE TO RETURN HOME... MY WIFE IS WAITING FOR ME.
YOU ARE LEAVING? BUT YOU HAVE JUST ARRIVED!
YOU ARE TIRED AND YOUR WIFE IS WAITING FOR YOU? SOMETHING TELLS ME THAT WILL NOT END WELL!
I KNOW... I AM JUST... TIRED.
HAHAHA!
HUH? WHERE IS THE SOLDIER? EVERYONE HAS DISAPPEARED!
EHH, THESE YOUNG PEOPLE! THEY DO NOT KNOW HOW TO HAVE FUN!
34

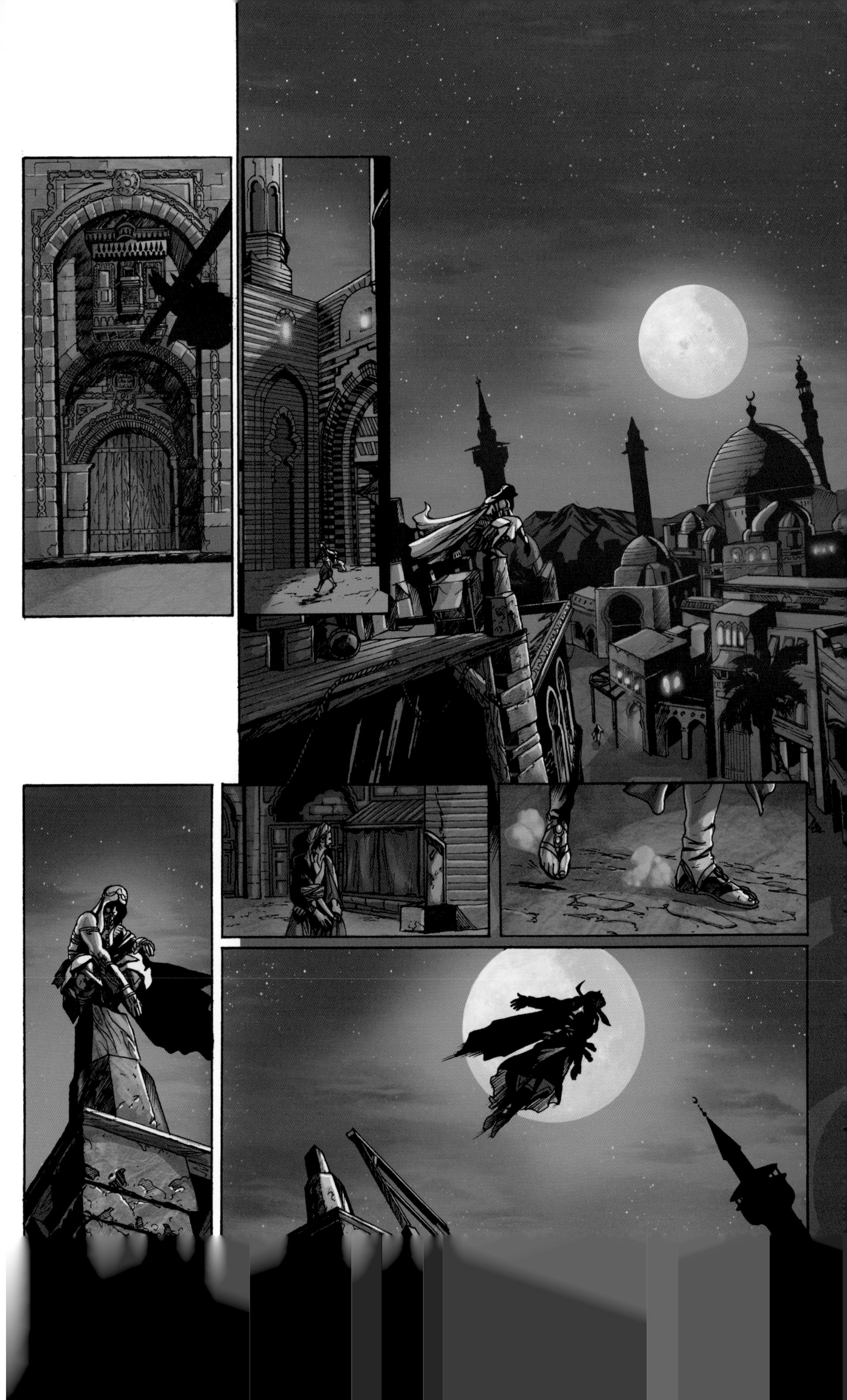

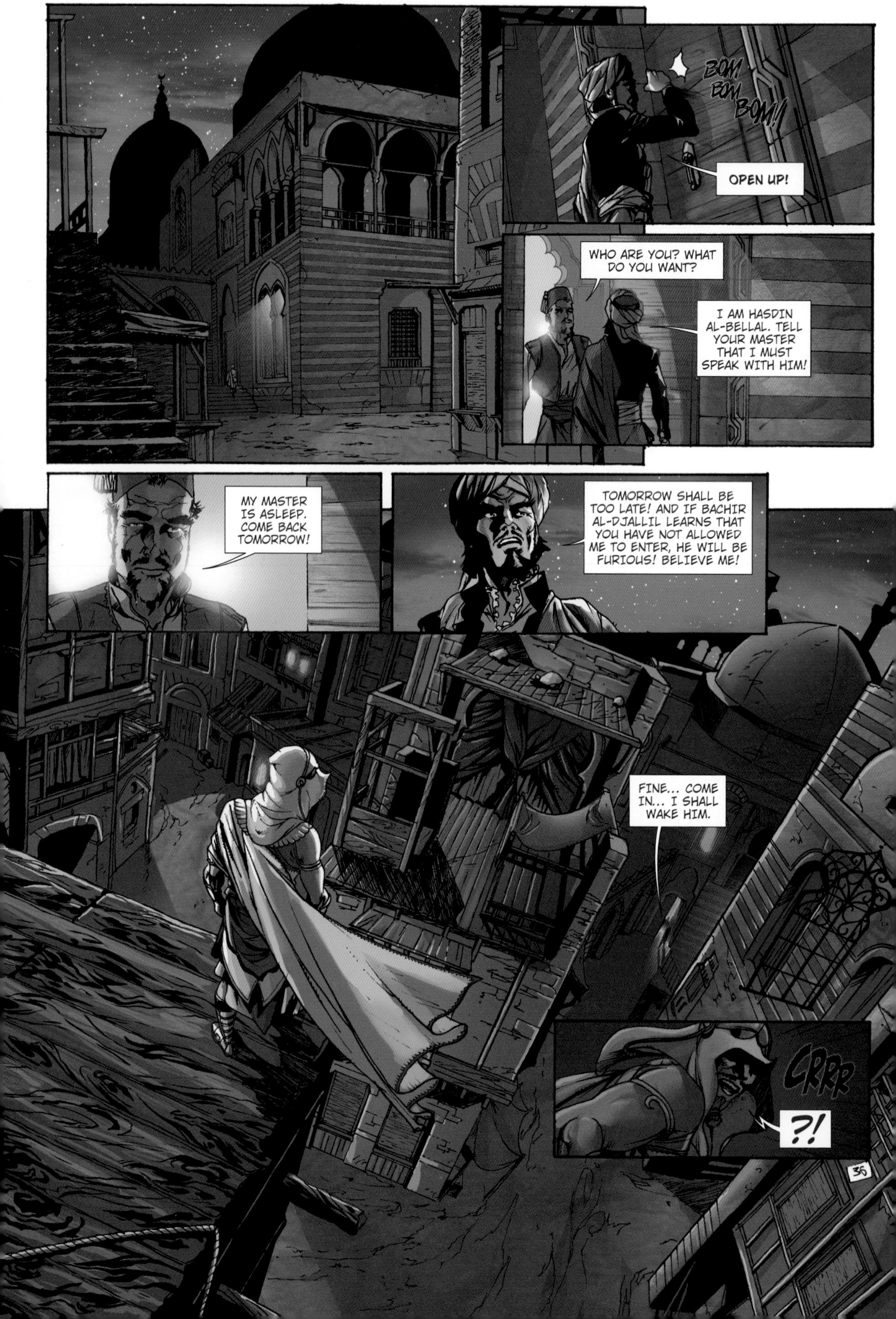
BOM BOM BOM!!
OPEN UP!
WHO ARE YOU? WHAT DO YOU WANT?
I AM HASDIN AL-BELLAL. TELL YOUR MASTER THAT I MUST SPEAK WITH HIM!
MY MASTER IS ASLEEP. COME BACK TOMORROW!
TOMORROW SHALL BE TOO LATE! AND IF BACHIR AL-DJALLIL LEARNS THAT YOU HAVE NOT ALLOWED ME TO ENTER, HE WILL BE FURIOUS! BELIEVE ME!
FINE... COME IN... I SHALL WAKE HIM.
CRRR
?!

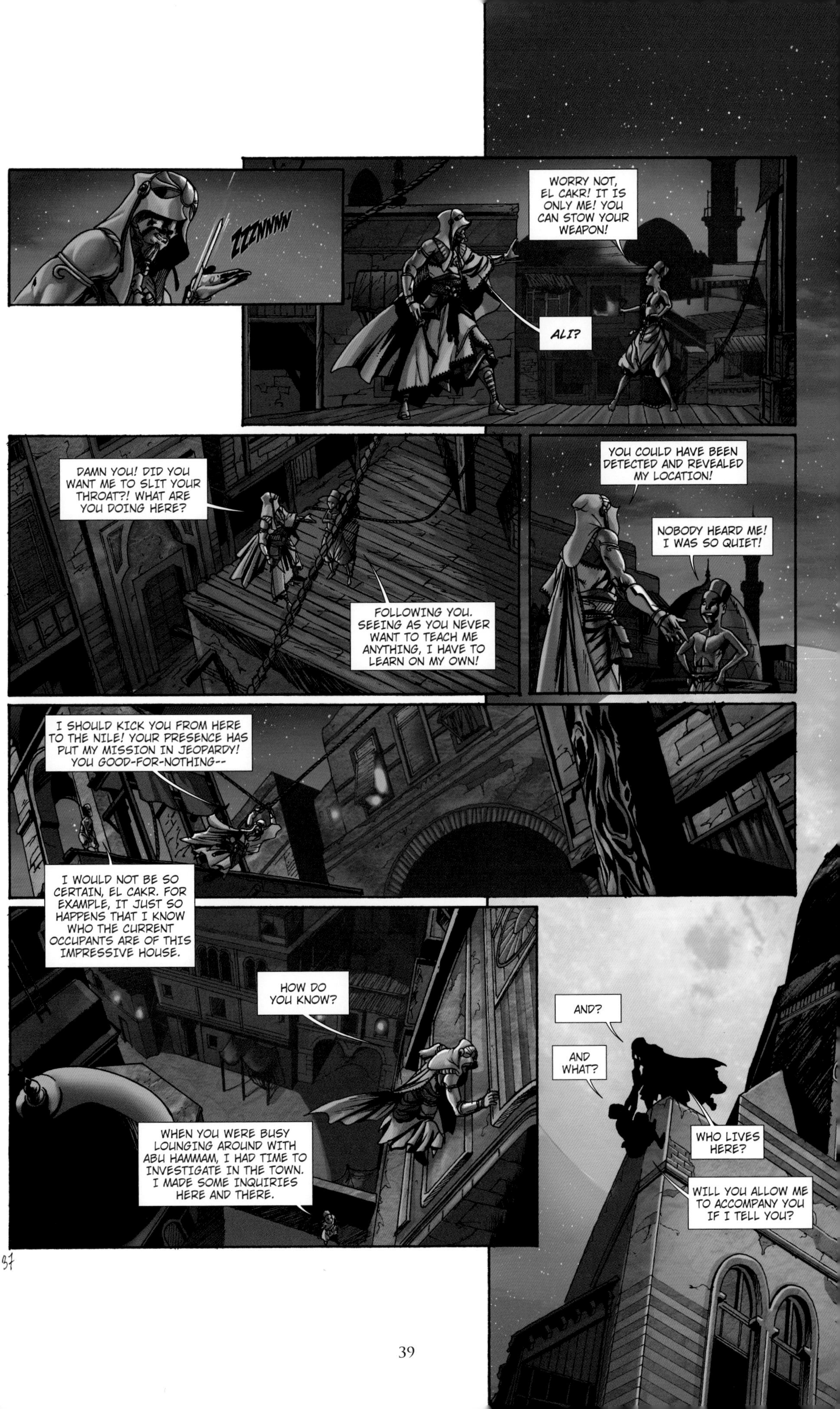
ZZZNNNN
WORRY NOT, EL CAKR! IT IS ONLY ME! YOU CAN STOW YOUR WEAPON!
ALI?
DAMN YOU! DID YOU WANT ME TO SLIT YOUR THROAT?! WHAT ARE YOU DOING HERE?
FOLLOWING YOU. SEEING AS YOU NEVER WANT TO TEACH ME ANYTHING, I HAVE TO LEARN ON MY OWN!
YOU COULD HAVE BEEN DETECTED AND REVEALED MY LOCATION!
NOBODY HEARD ME! I WAS SO QUIET!
I SHOULD KICK YOU FROM HERE TO THE NILE! YOUR PRESENCE HAS PUT MY MISSION IN JEOPARDY! YOU GOOD-FOR-NOTHING--
I WOULD NOT BE SO CERTAIN, EL CAKR. FOR EXAMPLE, IT JUST SO HAPPENS THAT I KNOW WHO THE CURRENT OCCUPANTS ARE OF THIS IMPRESSIVE HOUSE.
HOW DO YOU KNOW?
WHEN YOU WERE BUSY LOUNGING AROUND WITH ABU HAMMAM, I HAD TIME TO INVESTIGATE IN THE TOWN. I MADE SOME INQUIRIES HERE AND THERE.
AND?
AND WHAT?
WHO LIVES HERE?
WILL YOU ALLOW ME TO ACCOMPANY YOU IF I TELL YOU?
37

BLACKMAIL, ALI? NO, IT IS OUT OF THE QUESTION!

FINE, THEN I SHALL TELL YOU NOTHING...

STUBBORN URCHIN! VERY WELL, YOU MAY COME.

YES!

PROMISE?

HIS NAME IS BACHIR AL-DJALLIL, AN IMMENSELY RICH MARKET TRADER. HALF OF THE TOWN'S SILK RESERVES BELONG TO HIM.

BUT HE ALSO HAS A TASTE FOR FRESH MEAT...

WHAT DO YOU MEAN?

HE IS A VILE BEING. SOMEONE TOLD ME THAT HE HAS RAPED AND KILLED DOZENS OF YOUNG WOMEN.

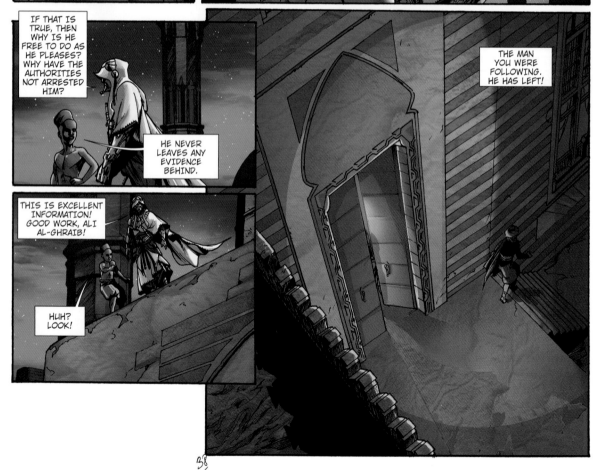

IF THAT IS TRUE, THEN WHY IS HE FREE TO DO AS HE PLEASES? WHY HAVE THE AUTHORITIES NOT ARRESTED HIM?

HE NEVER LEAVES ANY EVIDENCE BEHIND.

THE MAN YOU WERE FOLLOWING. HE HAS LEFT!

THIS IS EXCELLENT INFORMATION! GOOD WORK, ALI AL-GHRAIB!

HUH? LOOK!

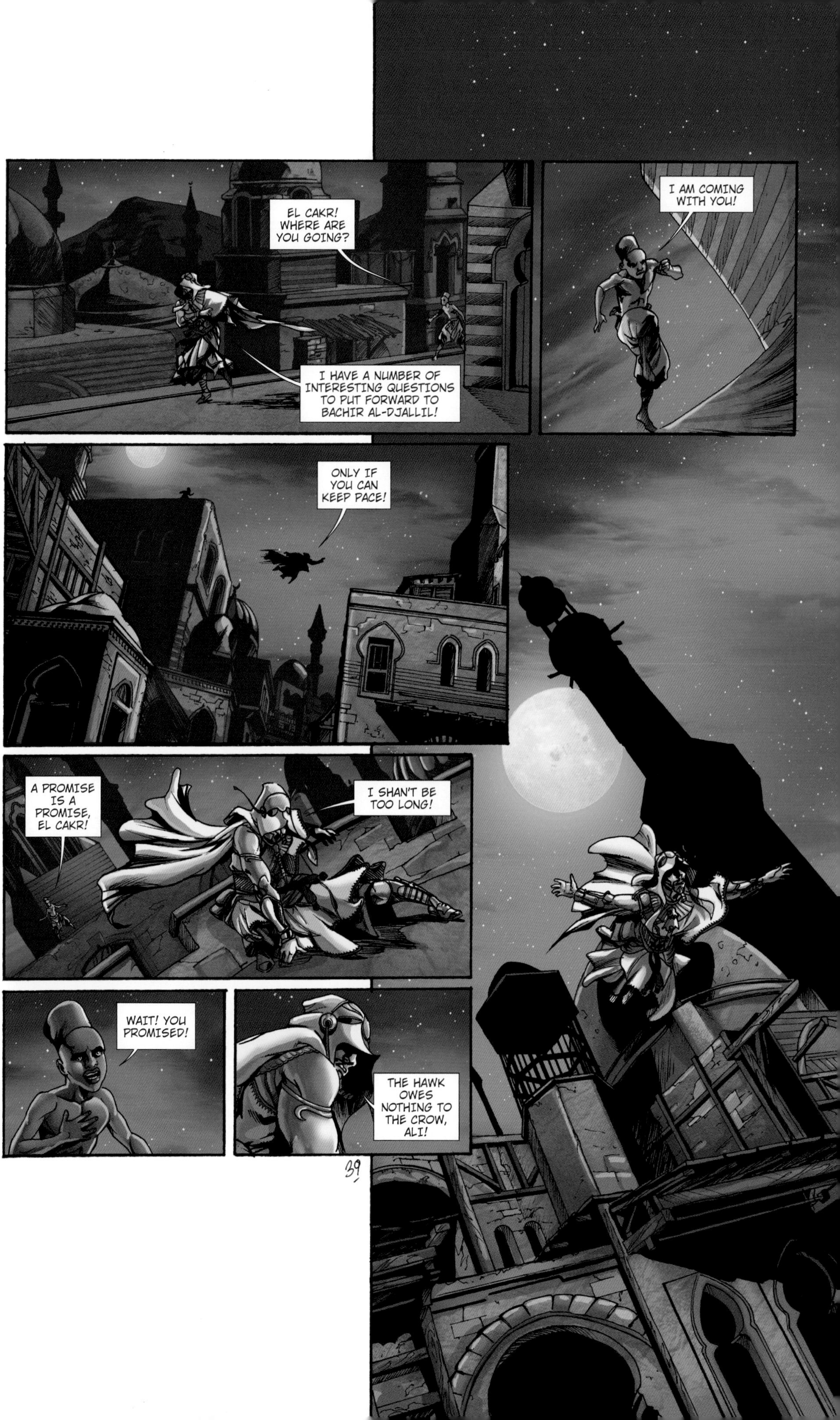
EL CAKR! WHERE ARE YOU GOING?
I HAVE A NUMBER OF INTERESTING QUESTIONS TO PUT FORWARD TO BACHIR AL-DJALLIL!
I AM COMING WITH YOU!
ONLY IF YOU CAN KEEP PACE!
A PROMISE IS A PROMISE, EL CAKR!
I SHAN'T BE TOO LONG!
WAIT! YOU PROMISED!
THE HAWK OWES NOTHING TO THE CROW, ALI!

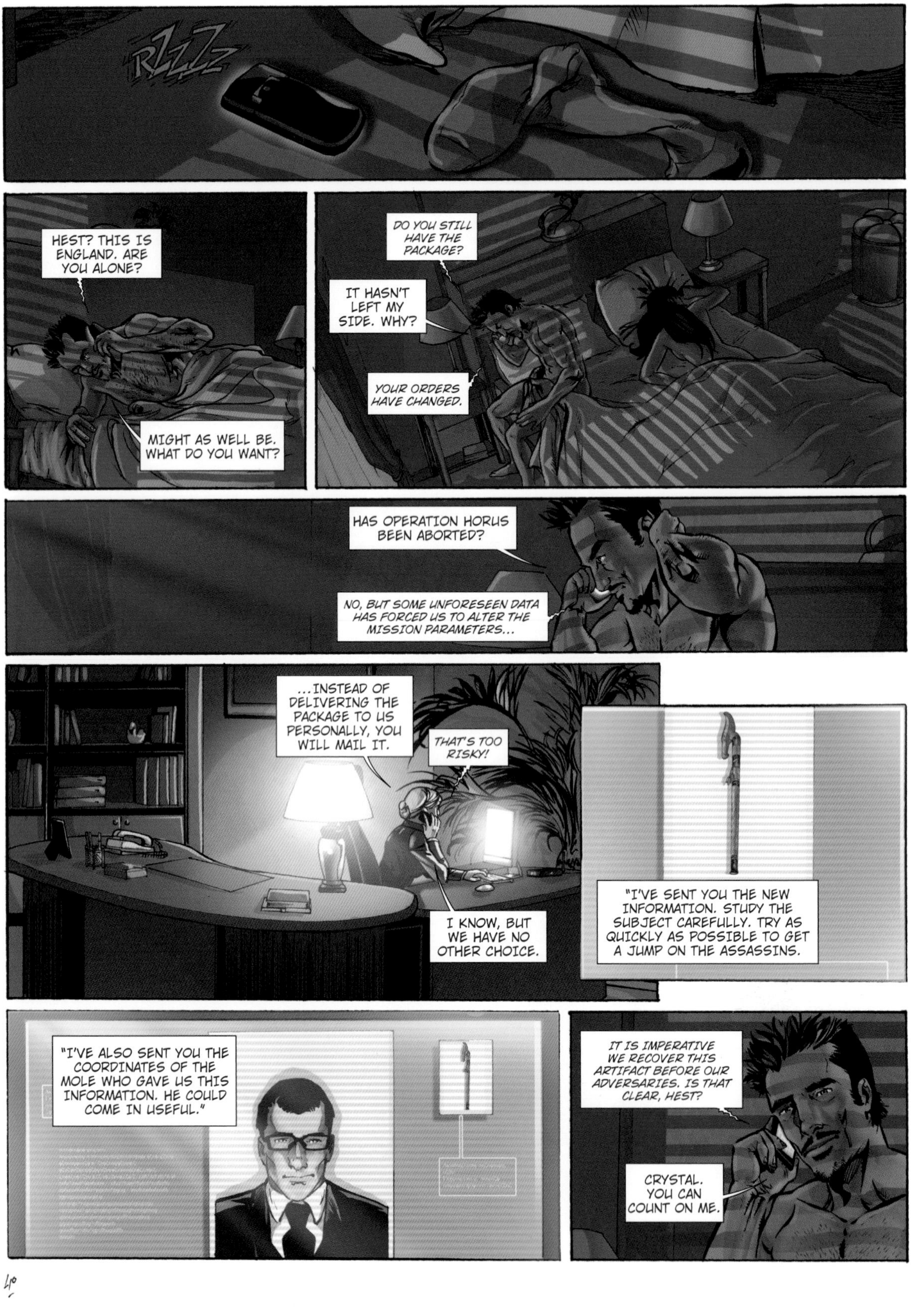
RZZZZ
HEST? THIS IS ENGLAND. ARE YOU ALONE?
MIGHT AS WELL BE. WHAT DO YOU WANT?
DO YOU STILL HAVE THE PACKAGE?
IT HASN'T LEFT MY SIDE. WHY?
YOUR ORDERS HAVE CHANGED.
HAS OPERATION HORUS BEEN ABORTED?
NO, BUT SOME UNFORESEEN DATA HAS FORCED US TO ALTER THE MISSION PARAMETERS...
...INSTEAD OF DELIVERING THE PACKAGE TO US PERSONALLY, YOU WILL MAIL IT.
THAT'S TOO RISKY!
I KNOW, BUT WE HAVE NO OTHER CHOICE.
"I'VE SENT YOU THE NEW INFORMATION. STUDY THE SUBJECT CAREFULLY. TRY AS QUICKLY AS POSSIBLE TO GET A JUMP ON THE ASSASSINS.
"I'VE ALSO SENT YOU THE COORDINATES OF THE MOLE WHO GAVE US THIS INFORMATION. HE COULD COME IN USEFUL."
IT IS IMPERATIVE WE RECOVER THIS ARTIFACT BEFORE OUR ADVERSARIES. IS THAT CLEAR, HEST?
CRYSTAL. YOU CAN COUNT ON ME.

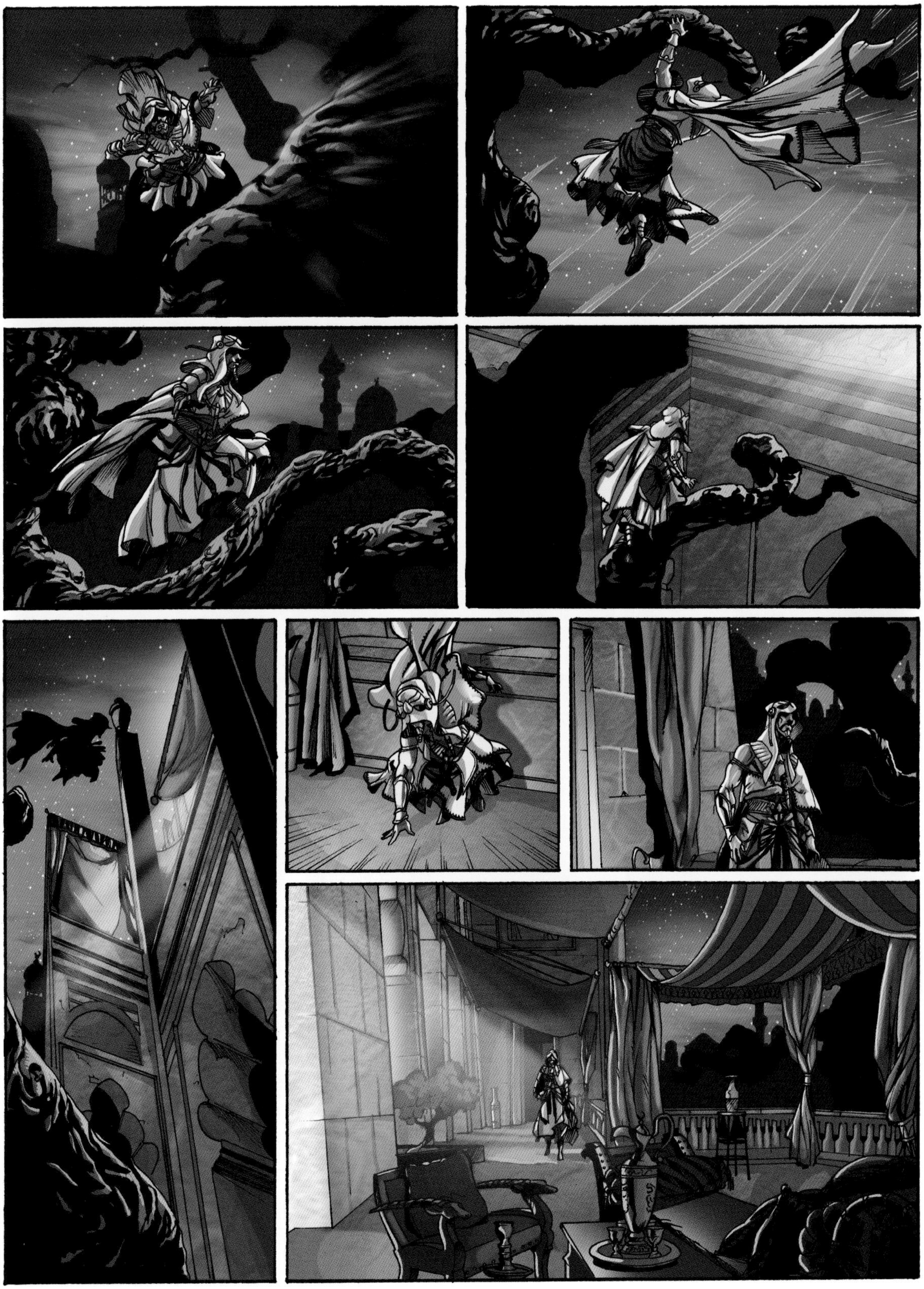

41

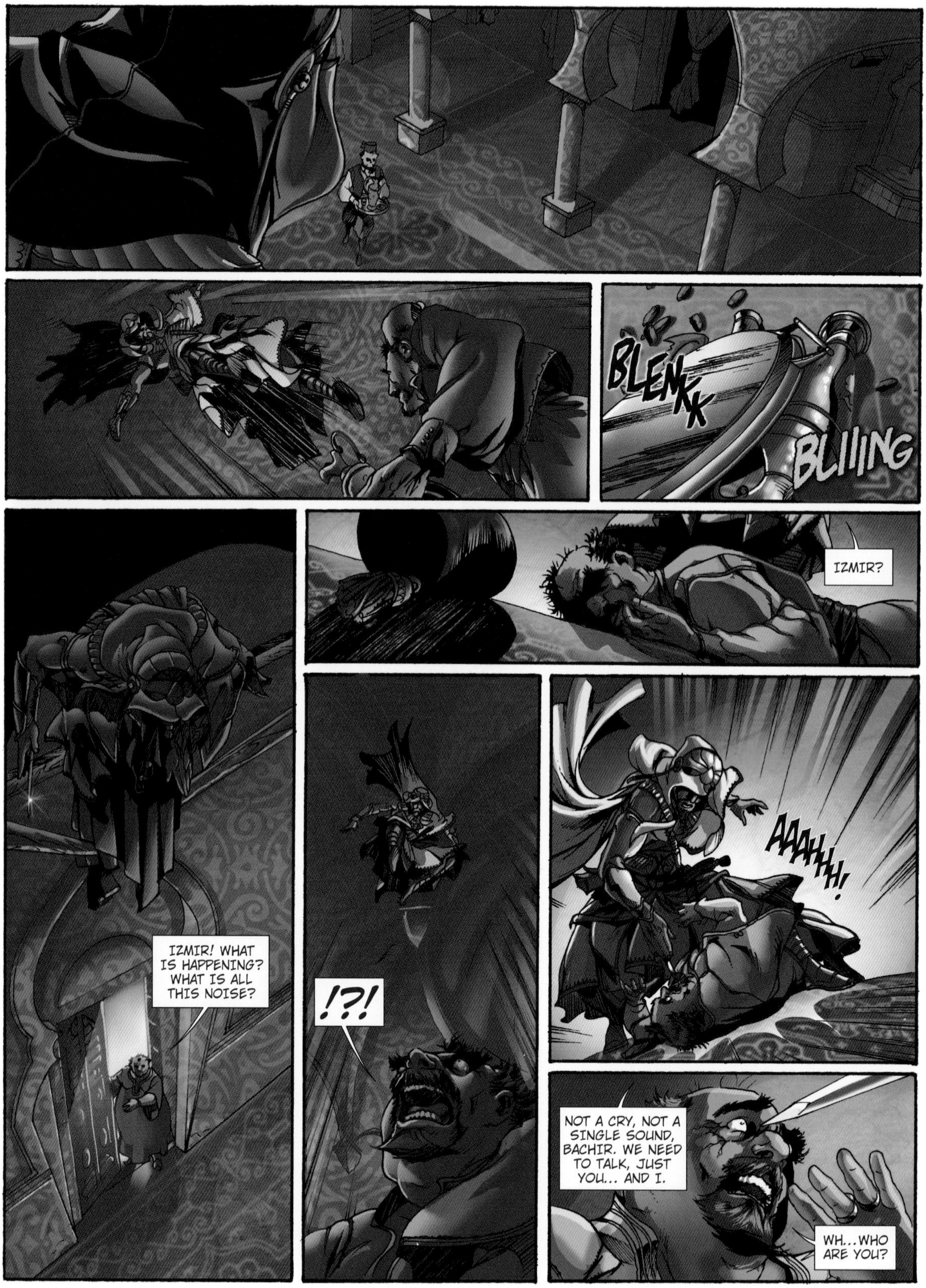
BLENKK
BLIIING
IZMIR?
IZMIR! WHAT IS HAPPENING? WHAT IS ALL THIS NOISE?
!?!
AAAHHH!
NOT A CRY, NOT A SINGLE SOUND, BACHIR. WE NEED TO TALK, JUST YOU... AND I.
WH...WHO ARE YOU?
42

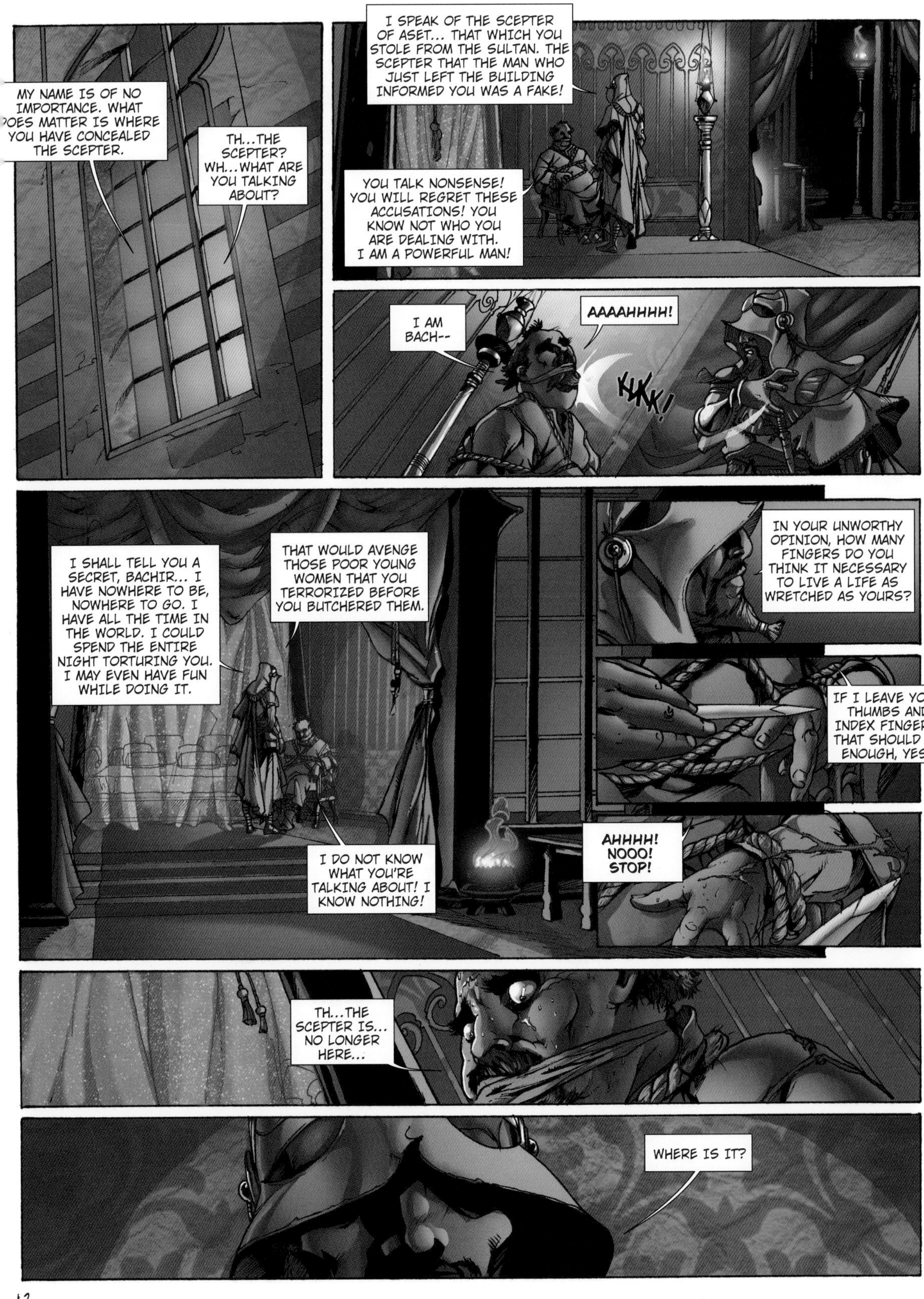
MY NAME IS OF NO IMPORTANCE. WHAT DOES MATTER IS WHERE YOU HAVE CONCEALED THE SCEPTER.
TH...THE SCEPTER? WH...WHAT ARE YOU TALKING ABOUT?
I SPEAK OF THE SCEPTER OF ASET... THAT WHICH YOU STOLE FROM THE SULTAN. THE SCEPTER THAT THE MAN WHO JUST LEFT THE BUILDING INFORMED YOU WAS A FAKE!
YOU TALK NONSENSE! YOU WILL REGRET THESE ACCUSATIONS! YOU KNOW NOT WHO YOU ARE DEALING WITH. I AM A POWERFUL MAN!
I AM BACH--
AAAAHHHH!
KLIKK!
I SHALL TELL YOU A SECRET, BACHIR... I HAVE NOWHERE TO BE, NOWHERE TO GO. I HAVE ALL THE TIME IN THE WORLD. I COULD SPEND THE ENTIRE NIGHT TORTURING YOU. I MAY EVEN HAVE FUN WHILE DOING IT.
THAT WOULD AVENGE THOSE POOR YOUNG WOMEN THAT YOU TERRORIZED BEFORE YOU BUTCHERED THEM.
I DO NOT KNOW WHAT YOU'RE TALKING ABOUT! I KNOW NOTHING!
IN YOUR UNWORTHY OPINION, HOW MANY FINGERS DO YOU THINK IT NECESSARY TO LIVE A LIFE AS WRETCHED AS YOURS?
IF I LEAVE YOUR THUMBS AND INDEX FINGERS, THAT SHOULD BE ENOUGH, YES?
AHHHH! NOOO! STOP!
TH...THE SCEPTER IS... NO LONGER HERE...
WHERE IS IT?
43

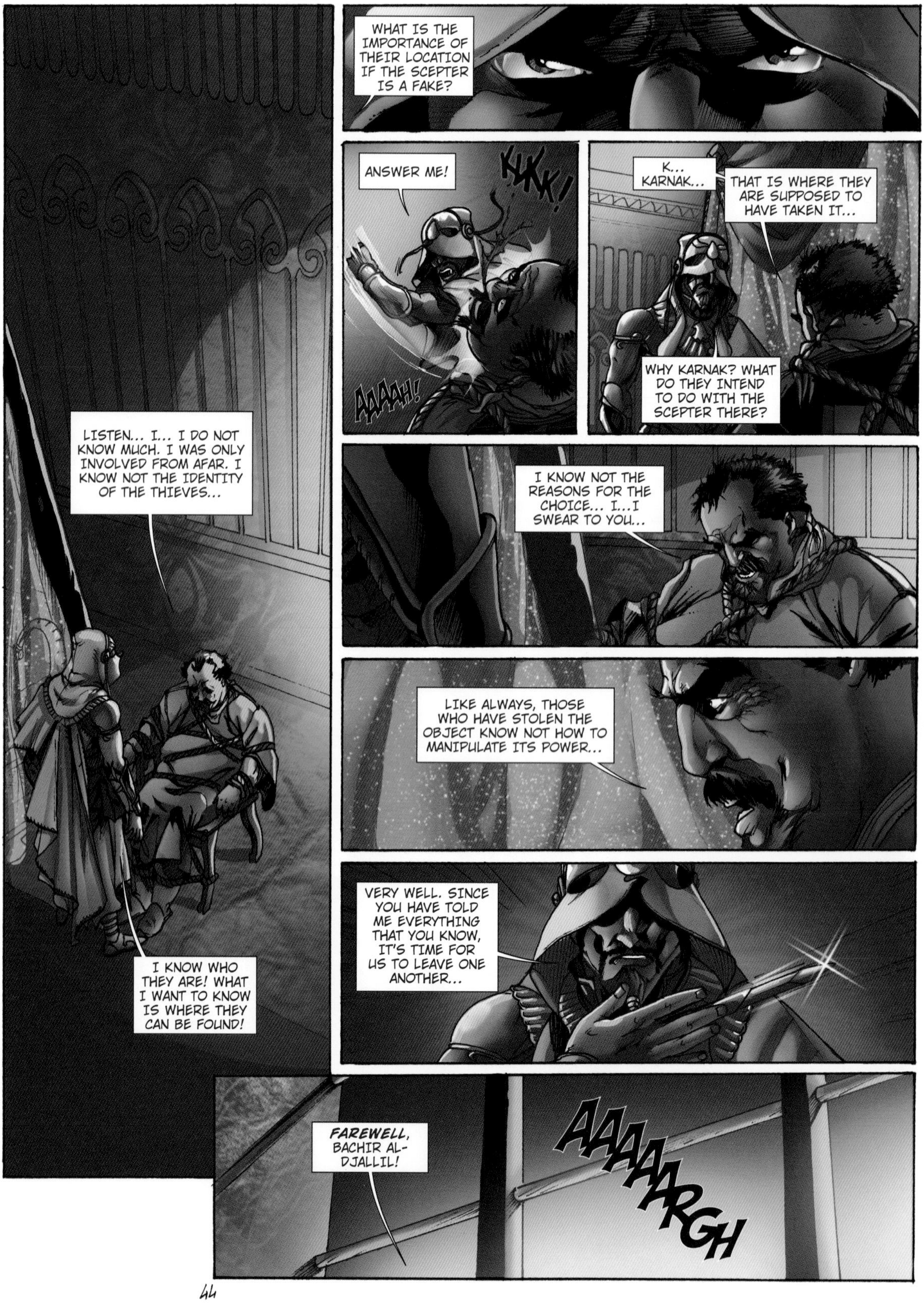
LISTEN... I... I DO NOT KNOW MUCH. I WAS ONLY INVOLVED FROM AFAR. I KNOW NOT THE IDENTITY OF THE THIEVES...
I KNOW WHO THEY ARE! WHAT I WANT TO KNOW IS WHERE THEY CAN BE FOUND!
WHAT IS THE IMPORTANCE OF THEIR LOCATION IF THE SCEPTER IS A FAKE?
ANSWER ME!
KKKK!
AAAAH!
K... KARNAK...
THAT IS WHERE THEY ARE SUPPOSED TO HAVE TAKEN IT...
WHY KARNAK? WHAT DO THEY INTEND TO DO WITH THE SCEPTER THERE?
I KNOW NOT THE REASONS FOR THE CHOICE... I...I SWEAR TO YOU...
LIKE ALWAYS, THOSE WHO HAVE STOLEN THE OBJECT KNOW NOT HOW TO MANIPULATE ITS POWER...
VERY WELL. SINCE YOU HAVE TOLD ME EVERYTHING THAT YOU KNOW, IT'S TIME FOR US TO LEAVE ONE ANOTHER...
FAREWELL, BACHIR AL-DJALLIL!
AAAAARGH

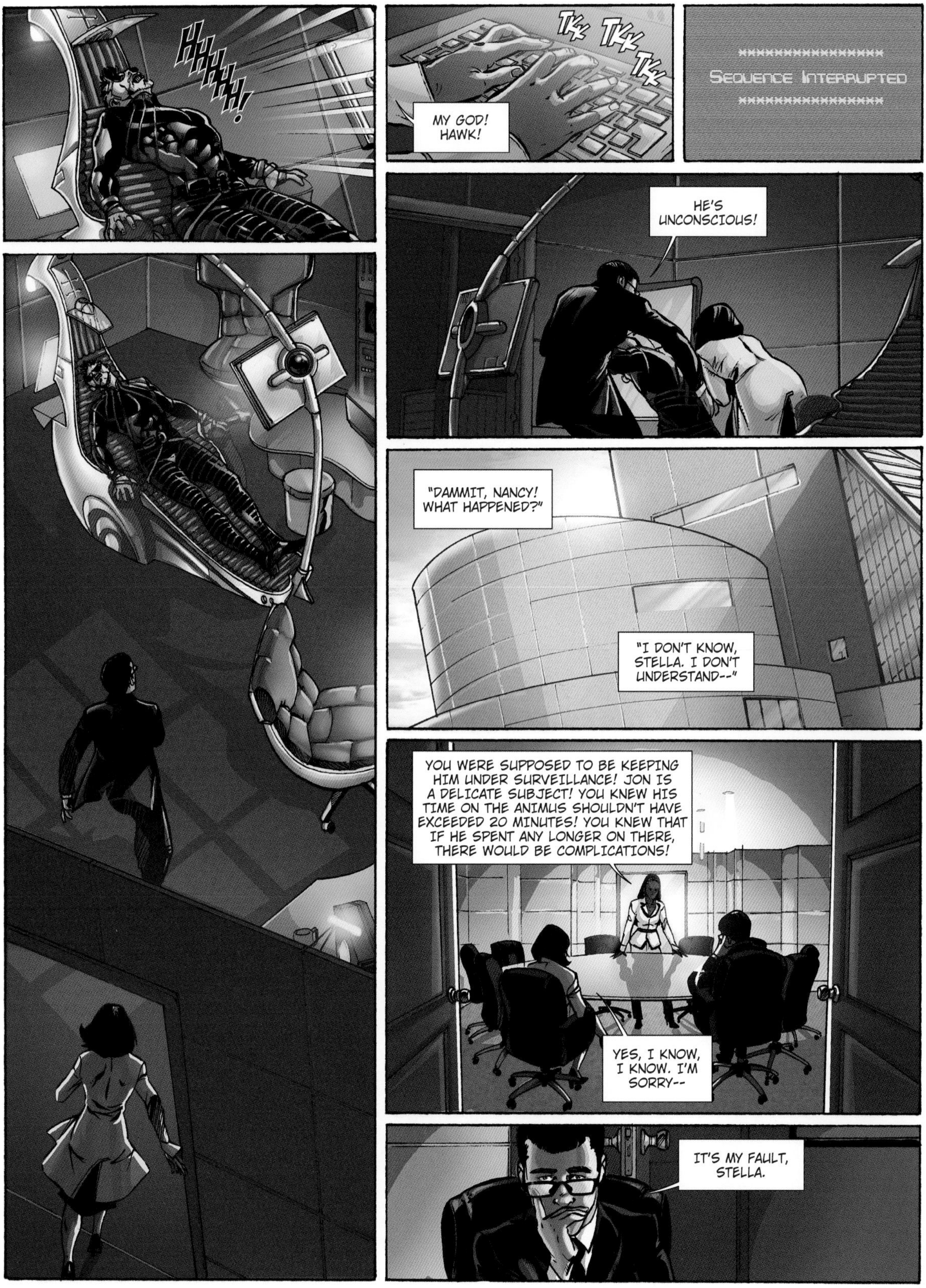
HHHHH!
TKK TKK TKK
MY GOD! HAWK!
SEQUENCE INTERRUPTED
HE'S UNCONSCIOUS!
"DAMMIT, NANCY! WHAT HAPPENED?"
"I DON'T KNOW, STELLA. I DON'T UNDERSTAND--"
YOU WERE SUPPOSED TO BE KEEPING HIM UNDER SURVEILLANCE! JON IS A DELICATE SUBJECT! YOU KNEW HIS TIME ON THE ANIMUS SHOULDN'T HAVE EXCEEDED 20 MINUTES! YOU KNEW THAT IF HE SPENT ANY LONGER ON THERE, THERE WOULD BE COMPLICATIONS!
YES, I KNOW, I KNOW. I'M SORRY--
IT'S MY FAULT, STELLA.

45

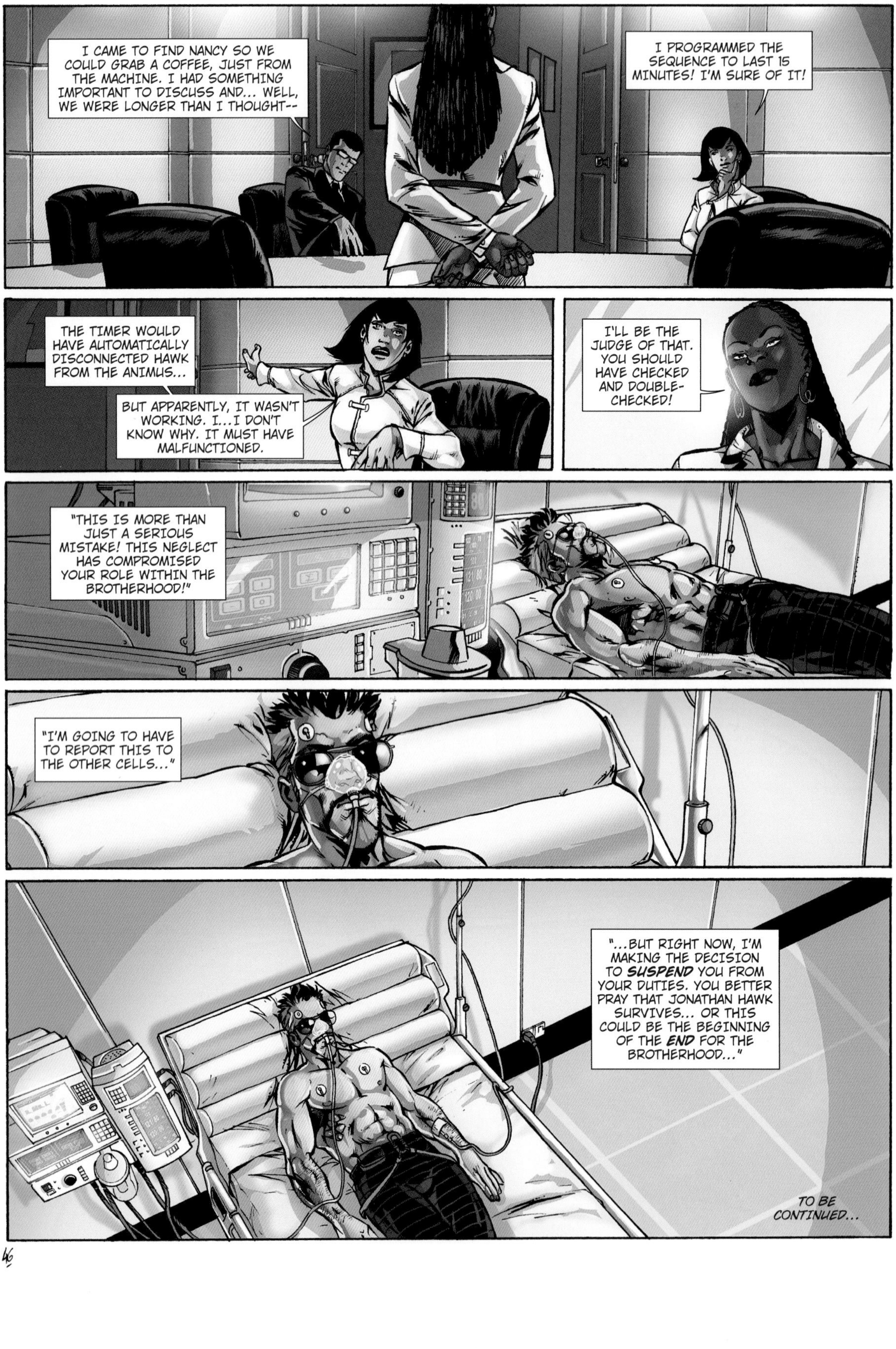
I CAME TO FIND NANCY SO WE COULD GRAB A COFFEE, JUST FROM THE MACHINE. I HAD SOMETHING IMPORTANT TO DISCUSS AND... WELL, WE WERE LONGER THAN I THOUGHT--
I PROGRAMMED THE SEQUENCE TO LAST 15 MINUTES! I'M SURE OF IT!
THE TIMER WOULD HAVE AUTOMATICALLY DISCONNECTED HAWK FROM THE ANIMUS...
BUT APPARENTLY, IT WASN'T WORKING. I...I DON'T KNOW WHY. IT MUST HAVE MALFUNCTIONED.
I'LL BE THE JUDGE OF THAT. YOU SHOULD HAVE CHECKED AND DOUBLE-CHECKED!
"THIS IS MORE THAN JUST A SERIOUS MISTAKE! THIS NEGLECT HAS COMPROMISED YOUR ROLE WITHIN THE BROTHERHOOD!"
"I'M GOING TO HAVE TO REPORT THIS TO THE OTHER CELLS..."
"...BUT RIGHT NOW, I'M MAKING THE DECISION TO **SUSPEND** YOU FROM YOUR DUTIES. YOU BETTER PRAY THAT JONATHAN HAWK SURVIVES... OR THIS COULD BE THE BEGINNING OF THE **END** FOR THE BROTHERHOOD..."
TO BE CONTINUED...
46